WHEN PARENTS TEXT

So Much Said . . . So Little Understood

LAUREN
KAELIN
SOPHIA
FRAIOLI

WORKMAN PUBLISHING • NEW YORK

To Mama and Papa K, without your ceaseless support none of this would be possible.—lk

To Mom and Dad, you've shaped the person I've become. Thank you for all your love and support. I love you very much.—sf

<3

Copyright © 2011 by Lauren Kaelin and Sophia Fraioli
Design copyright © by Workman Publishing

Library of Congress Cataloging-in-Publication Data

Kaelin, Lauren.
When parents text : so much said . . . so little understood /
Lauren Kaelin and Sophia Fraioli.
p. cm.
ISBN 978-0-7611-6604-7 (alk. paper)
1. Text messages (Telephone systems)--Humor. 2. Parenting--Humor.
I. Fraioli, Sophia. II. Title.
PN6231.T565K34 2011
384.5'34--dc23

Cover design by Will Staehle with Jean-Marc Troadec
Cover photo by Thomas Northcut/Getty Images
Interior design by Jean-Marc Troadec
Illustrations by Tae Won Yu

Workman books are available at special discounts when purchased in bulk for premiums and sales promotions as well as for fund-raising or educational use. Special editions or book excerpts also can be created to specification. For details, contact the Special Sales Director at the address below, or send an e-mail to specialmarkets@workman.com.

Workman Publishing Company, Inc.
225 Varick Street
New York, NY 10014-4381
www.workman.com

Printed in the United States of America

First printing August 2011

10 9 8 7 6 5 4 3 2

CONTENTS

INTRODUCTION

When Parents Text, in some ways, is about us—recent graduates, home from college, best friends for life. But it's also about a generational divide—a technology gap between parents and their children. There is a new code of our generation, one of tweets, likes, and appropriately placed emoticons. We wrote the rule book, and now our parents are trying to learn the rules.

Our website was originally about our parents: our mothers and fathers, our muses. It was about how much we love them and how crazy they are. It has now become, we hope, about your family—how much you love them and how crazy they are. It has been our privilege to read the exchanges between parents and children and see glimpses of our own in them. Some people worry that technology is hindering human connection, creating more distance in relationships, but we think *When Parents Text* is evidence to the contrary.

We hope that our website has brought you joy, made you LOL, and finally opened some dialogue about the meaning of the word *chode*.

Best of luck in your future communicative struggles.

We met in elementary school and bonded over mutual love for soccer and trading Got Milk? ads during recess. When we entered sixth grade, we sat next to each other in social studies class and became best friends.

It was 1999: Our most prized possessions were our portable Discmans. We spent countless hours downloading music from Napster while communicating incessantly over AOL Instant Messenger on our parents' desktop computers. We did not own cell phones until the end of high school (and we're sure those first few texts would be worthy of a website).

We were inseparable throughout high school, contenders for the dynamic duo superlative; most people still think we're sisters. Despite all this, we come from very different families.

Lauren: If you call my house in Montclair, New Jersey, a four-year-old me with a subtle lisp will tell you that you've reached the Kaelins and you can "leave a message, if you like." For twenty years, that has been the message on our answering machine. And when my parents eventually retire and hopefully move to their dream lakeshore property, I'm sure they'll find a way to take it with them.

I grew up the youngest of three in a fairly traditional household. For two decades, my home hasn't changed much, sporting the same floral wallpaper, upholstered couches, and linoleum countertops. My mother diligently changes our holiday decorations–from pumpkins to Santas to snowmen to hearts. My father loyally watches the Knicks games and completes *The New York Times* crossword puzzle Sunday through Wednesday.

To combat our Catholic upbringing and strict curfews, my brother, sister, and I snuck copious amounts of music television and late-night phone calls. We developed sarcastic personalities and fairly foul mouths.

I went to Smith College, a small women's school in the Pioneer Valley of Massachusetts with a legacy-rich history. "Barbara Bush drank tea on this couch." "Betty Friedan lived in that house." My college experience was the perfect mixture of baby grand pianos, hundred-year-old tradition, and modern debauchery.

When I graduated, I was told I could do anything: follow in the paths of notable alumnae, tackle the issues, lead a life of distinction. I did not spend four years trying to figure out what to do when I graduated, but convincing myself I never would. I had bought the GRE prep book but had stopped at the chapter on

Special Right Triangles and opted instead to perfect my gin and tonic proportions.

Come graduation, I was ceremoniously booted into the real world. With few job prospects and overwhelming student loans, I returned to my suburban home and all its familiarities.

In this childhood redux, I no longer have to sneak music television, but actively tune in for *Jersey Shore*. When I come home at 3 A.M., my mom asks me to walk more quietly. It's ideal, really–homemade soups, live-in laundry, and the most obliging of roommates.

Sophia: The Fraiolis would best be described as loud. Loud voices, loud opinions, and loud personalities. We are a middle-class family, Jewish, Italian, and a little bit crazy.

I come from a long line of New Jerseyians. My mom was from Trenton, and my dad lived in a small town called Essex Fells, and before that, my mother's parents both came from South Jersey. I was born in New York City, but after four years of life in Manhattan, the Garden State seemed to be calling my family's name. So we decided to leave our apartment in the East Village and move to Montclair, New Jersey, the sixth borough of New York.

I grew up the way most kids did in my town. My sister and I attended public school and spent Mondays and Wednesdays learning Hebrew at our local temple. My life played out in typical suburban fashion. I sang and danced in school plays and made macaroni necklaces in art class. I spent my teen years being clumsy and very messy. I rarely cleaned my room and had my friends write lyrics on my walls in permanent marker.

In the summer, I vacationed on Martha's Vineyard, where I spent full days with my extended family on the beach, followed by hefty barbecued meals prepared by my father. When I finally graduated from high school, I was excited to move beyond the suburban landscape I had grown up in and on to something more exciting.

I decided to attend the University of Vermont, where I studied anthropology and political science. I went to a lot of parties and switched roommates more times than I'd care to recall. I gained an amazing group of friends and by my junior year could call the small city of Burlington my home. But at the end of my four years, I sat among my classmates at graduation with no plan. Lauren and I had discussed the prospect of moving south, somewhere warm where we could live together, but neither of us had the means to do it.

Like many recent graduates, my only option was to move back home.

Though I felt slightly defeated, I knew that Lauren and a handful of my other friends from high school would be there, too. And we could commiserate about failed job interviews and the woes of parental problems together.

Reestablishing this relationship with my mom and dad was not easy. But after a while, we came to an understanding about when I needed to do the dishes and how my previous curfew of midnight was no longer acceptable. We can now agree on scheduling our DVR properly and eat dinner together on most nights.

We never imagined the adult version of our friendship playing out back in our hometown. It's strange living at home and not having to wake up for school in the morning, not caring whether or not it's a snow day. It was a postgraduate twist neither of us expected. But there were also reassuring consistencies: a few old friends, the local deli, real bagels, and the new joys of our favorite bar.

In between babysitting jobs, unpaid internships, e-mails from DirectLoans, and taking NJ Transit into the city for various hourly wages, we received some texts from our parents.

THE ORIGIN STORY

Lauren already had had tacos for dinner, but Sophia hadn't eaten since lunch, so she insisted on stopping at a Panera for a soup-and-salad combo before going out to meet friends. It was near closing time. As the staff mopped around the soda machine and Sophia ate her Fuji Apple Chicken Salad and artisan bread, a fateful exchange took place.

"You have to see this text my mom sent me today," Lauren said.

Sophia looked at Lauren's phone and laughed. "When parents text, it's hilarious," she said.

"That should be a website."

The next day we registered a domain name and started collecting texts from our siblings and friends. "We're starting a website! It's called When Parents Text."

These next pages are some of the first posts from our site. If you haven't traveled back this far in the archives, please enjoy our humble beginnings.

Tacos for Dinner

MOM: Tacos or meat loaf for dinner?

ME: Tacos

MOM: Bring your appetite. When will you be home?

MOM: Eta?

MOM: ???

ME: Can you pick me up at 6:45? My phone is going to die.

MOM: Walnut St?

ME: Yes

MOM: How many tacos?

ME: Might be more like 7.

MOM: Tacos?

ME: No, my train gets in then.

ME: Tacos? 2?

MOM: How many tacos?

ME: Mom, chill with the tacos.

Empty Fridge

ME: Is there anything to eat at home?

MOM: Bean corn

From the Grave

MOM: Aunt Mary Louise passed

Old but Relevant

MOM: michael jackson died

ME: i know!! its so crazy

MOM: i still cant believe it.

MOM: people die, everyday.

Did You Mean "Referral"?

MOM: I just picked up the reefer. All there. Is lots of traffic. Call the doctor to see if you can reschedule for another day.

Speak to Text

MOM: wanted to know to plan for dinner we are having depression chili I m using speak dear bish yes chile picturing you will be very good this is good for many laughs the dinner we'll be d d licious

Delightful

ME: You smell

DAD: Like a sweet summer's breeze

1:59 A.M.

MOM: Time to be home.

Precisely

MOM: Happy Birthday! You were born at 3:59 PM. I remember it very clearly. I loved you from the first second.

Ed

ME: The eye exam costs 35 so I hope they take my card because I don't have cash.

DAD: U r Ok. i called. Ed

ME: Ok. you don't need to sign messages 'ed' every time you send them.

DAD: It happens automatically.

ME: But sometimes you sign 'dad'

DAD: Thats when I remember to type Dad. But u kno who i am. Ed

Hurricane Prep

MOM: It's kind of windy? Aunt Lu says she filled the bathtub with water and has plenty of vodka. Cousin Fred is there.

Saturday Morning

MOM: BEAUTIFUL DAY!!! Get and up & enjoy it!

MOM: Wake up, get out of bed!

MOM: GET UP!!!! ARE YOU MISSING IT!!!

More Like the Parental Network

ME: Ugh, you never should have been given an iPhone

MOM: This is a wonderful way for me to keep in touch with you, do you want to be my Facebook friend?

ME: Nooo

MOM: I'll friend you

Non Sequitur

DAD: Public transport is where its at . . . your bro has a girlfriend named eileen.

That's One Fine Day

DAD: On train to see my eighth grade teacher - then a nun, now 73-year-old grandmother./ Tell me where you are

Table for One?

DAD: Dining alone

ME: Loser

DAD: Big time.

Mom's Got Jokes

MOM: What do you call a cow with no legs?

MOM: Ground Beef!!

Breakfast

MOM: Gritts eggs wild main blueberry with warm blueberry syrup pancakes tky sausage miss u how was ur nite

Phone Impostor

MOM: Are you not answering your phone?

MOM: Give me a sign that it's you!

ME: Are you serious?

Non Denominational

MOM: I FOUND YOUR WALLET!!!!!

ME: Praise Allah

MOM: God and St. Anthony

TEXTING: THE PHENOMENON

When Parents Text was originally about the trials and errors of parents handling cell phones, the meeting of small keypads and old hands. We hoped to document the hilarity of technology gaps between generations: T9, appropriate emoticons, and Facebook etiquette. Somewhere along the way, LOL became "lots of love," emoticons stopped expressing emotions, and texting became a format to ask unanswerable questions. Gradually our website became less about technological fumbles and more about relationships. Texting is now a way for parents to stay in touch with their kids, keep up to date on their locations, and remind them of mealtimes. Moreover, through texting, parents are able to instantly communicate their every thought, request, and question. A modern-day "wish you were here," texting between parents and their children is both hilarious and heartwarming.

nOObs

Lauren: The very first texts I received from my mother were simply "LK PHONE HOME," and then ten minutes later "LK PHONE HOME." Texting was coupled with Saturday morning phone calls and e-mails in all caps: "LAUREN CALL HOME."

When I did call home, concerned that something could be wrong, my mother told me that the caps were just to "make it stand out."

These next few pages show parents echoing my mother's first attempts at communication.

Hello

MOM: =

ME: haha what is that?

MOM: i dont know just saying hello

Fisheads

ME: Can you pick me up from the airport tomorrow?

DAD: Fisheads.

ME: What?

DAD: its my only saved quicktext.

Mom2Mom

MOM: Ok - we'll visit about it tomorrow. I love you!!

MOM: Love you, too, Mom!

Hamburger House

DAD: I'm going to drop off your dorm application. It's hamburger house right?

DAD: Hamburger

DAD: Hamburger

DAD: I don't know how this phone gets "hamburger" from H-a-r-d-i-n.

(one hour later)

DAD: Don't get your hopes up. They said hamburger house is basically already filled up.

DAD: Hamburger

DAD: Not again

Mavin

DAD: I have a text account now. I am a technology mavin. Have a good day

Multiple Choice

MOM: How are you :(or :)

Saying Words

MOM: My fingers are saying words. This is amazing.

Higgy Higgy

ME: hey mom

MOM: higgy higgy

ME: . . . umm what's that supposed to mean

MOM: oh sorry that was supposed to say hi how are you. i'm new at this

Abusing Quick Text

ME: Hey dad, when are you going to be home?

DAD: Let's meet up!

ME: Are you sending random quick texts again?

DAD: Let's meet up!

GGMM

MOM: Fantastic!! I am trying to work GGMM in to a text but haven't had the right context yet. Can you figure out what it is??

ME: Haha i have no clue . . .

MOM: One of my catch phrases . . . for showing shock or astonishment. You still don't know?

ME: Good god molly moses?

MOM: Would I say that!?! Good golly, Miss Molly!!

Eyepatch

MOM: When will you be home? ;)

ME: Pretty soon, why?

MOM: Just wondering ;) going to bed soon ;)

ME: Okay, what's with the winky face?

MOM: What?

ME: This! ;)

MOM: That's a pirate. See he has an eyepatch! ;) ;)

Big Ups

MOM: This is my very first text message. It's for Jesus!

Pepperoni

MOM: Is pepperoni coming over?

MOM: I mean Melanie.

FWD: HELLO!

DAD: Just wanted to say hello to you!!
<Subject: Fwd: FW: FWD: FW: FWD:
FWD: FWD: FW: FWD: FW>

DAD: what is a signature and how do i
<Subject: Fwd: FW: FWD: FW: FWD:
FWD: FWD: FW: FWD: FW>

DAD: change it?? <Subject: Fwd: FW: FWD:
FW: FWD: FWD: FWD: FW: FWD: FW>

:1)}

DAD: :l)}

ME: what??

DAD: this is me with my beard, I'm smiling.

Fast

DAD: Look how fast im texting!

Hugz from Dad, XO.

DAD: ({})

ME: What?!

DAD: It's a hug.

ME: . . . that doesn't mean what you think it means.

SUBJECT:

DAD: SUBJECT: sick.
MESSAGE: Your mother is vomit.

ME: Vomiting? And how do you even put in a subject?

Heartfelt Apology

DAD:Iwillpickitupforyou.iamsosorryforbeing meanandnotverycompasionate.Ihopeyouwill forgiveme.LoveDad

Camel Hoof

MOM: Ewww, this girl just had a camel hoof!

ME: Camel……toe?

Unread

DAD: What does "unread" mean on my messages?

ME: You haven't read it. . . .

Bloodwork

MOM: I've been farting all day because I have to get bloodwork done tomorrow.

ME: Did you mean fasting??

MOM: Oops. I meant to hit the button four times.

Susan Boyle at Rockefeller Center

MOM: What's the story??????

ME: Going out to dinner

MOM: Not to Susan Doyle?

ME: Boyle?

MOM: Doyle

MOM: The phone has a mind of it's own! Won't type B

MOM: It doesn't like Susan

MOM: It prefers Doyle

MOM: You try

ME: Boyle

Dickstain

MOM: i learned 2 txt!

(three hours later)

MOM: dickstain

F%#@ing Bus

ME: The bus was late today :(

DAD: F%#@ing bus!!!! Dont tbey know you have stuff to do??

ME: Haha you can type the word out, dad.

DAD: Thats too mainstream for me.

My Pin

DAD: what is the typey thing I do so we can be BBM friends?

ME: type my pin without a space in between

DAD: mypine

DAD: mypim_

DAD: my pin

DAD: it's not working.

ME: dad.... .

R2D2

ME: So are you advanced enough to text now daddy?

DAD: I'm working on it

(five minutes later)

DAD: I'm going to name this R 2 D 2

Finals

MOM: Hi. What are you doing?

ME: At the library studying for my organic chem exam.

MOM: Homo.

ME: Excuse me?

MOM: I meant to spell GOOD. sorry.

Skillz

MOM: I am sending a two handed text

Mad

MOM: COME HOME RIGHT NOW

MOM: COME HOME RIGHT NOW

MOM: COME HOME RIGHT NOW

MOM: COME HOME RIGHT NOW

MOM: COME HOME RIGHT NOW

MOM: COME HOME RIGHT NOW

ME: Okay . . . um why did you send me this 6 times?

MOM: i am mad

FML

ME: FML

MOM: what?

ME: Fuck my life

MOM: oh, I thought family medical leave haha

When Parents Watch TV

DAD: you broke the tv

ME: no i didnt

DAD: it wont work, I called comcast and set up an appointment

ME: did you try pressing the input button?

ME: . . .

DAD: sorry was on the phone with comcast, had to cancel appointment

I Love You, Dad

DAD: What does Totes Magoats* mean?

ME: Totally

DAD: Totally what?

ME: It's just an expression. Magoets rhymes with totes so people say it.

DAD: I think life is just passing me by

Made famous by Paul Rudd in the movie I Love You, Man.

Emoticon Madness

MOM: :() that's a monkey! -:), ME WITH ONE HAIR!

ME: hahahaha cool mommy

MOM: :#(SAD MAN WITH MUSTACHE. NOW ITS ALL AND I DONT KNOW HOW TO CHANGE IT.

Sneaking

ME: Can you still pick us up in a bit?

MOM: Wdp

ME: What?

(fifteen minutes later)

MOM: I was in a meeting and tried to type that under the desk. Thats hard to do. I didn't pres the keys enough. Wdp = yes

Pumpkin Bread

MOM: the text that i just sent u, i sent to the wrong person over an hour ago. I just found out cuz they sent me a text saying "i don't know who this is but good luck with the pumpkin bread."

Airplane Mode

MOM: How do I turn my phone off?

ME: Hold the red power button down. It's usually the end call button

MOM: I don't understand. I am getting on a plane. I don't want to cause a plane crash.

MOM: Hi this is Steve, your mom wanted to let you know she found help turning off her phone, she'll talk to you in 14 hours. Love you! (this is mom)

MPRNONG

ME: When do you want me to come?

MOM: 10:00 IN THE MPRNONG!

ME: Why are you yelling?

MOM: Not yelling. Just not good at texting.

Nothing Special

DAD: In order not to forget how to send text messages, I just practice sending it. There is nothing special. Pls ignore this text.

FLASH

DAD: ill send you a FLASH tomorrow

ME: What's a flash?

DAD: this thing that goes FLASH on the phone

ME: It's a text, thanks.

Voice Activation

MOM: milk orange juice fruit veggies creamer if it's on sale. Soup. Forget the soup I just sneezed And it is thought I said Soup. ####, ####. I just said that f word And the s word And it types Pound sign! My phone's a Train No it's not a train It's a pretty easy day No it's not A pretty easy day I never said that. I said my phone is a prude

Bluetooth

MOM: Its hard to do things while I'm talking on the phone. I think I need to get a blacktooth.

Helrp

DAD: Helrp my fimgers too big for kleypad. <:((

Vibrated

MOM: Your phone just vibrated.

MOM: It just did it again.

Lunch Maggots

MOM: Stop at dollar store on way home and get lunch maggots.

ME: Lunch maggots?

MOM: Baffles.

MOM: Baggies.

MOM: Ziplock lunch Baggies.

MOM: Spell check is not helping me.

MOM: This is dad by the way.

Sad Face

MOM: if I knew how to make a sad face I would place it here

@

DAD: can u buy milk

DAD: @ tea bags

ME: You know that @ means at and not and, right dad?

DAD: no

LOL

MOM: I thought LOL meant Little Old Lady

Favorite Words

DAD: Eyebrows

ME: What?! and since when do you know how to text?

DAD: Its mom now. Im teaching dad how to text and his favorite word is eyebrows

Funniest Home Videos

DAD: hello son. I need you to call me as soon as you get this. I am using good grammar because your mom said it bugs you when I dont. Sorry I didnt use an apostraphe I dont know how. I also dont know how to do a zero. I still use a capital O. Actually you dont have to call me anymore.

ME: how long did that take you to write?

DAD: lets just say funniest home videos is almost over.

Brb, Africa

MOM: Are you on your way to Zimbabwe?

MOM: Zimbabwe

MOM: Zimbabwe

MOM: Zimbabwe

MOM: zumba

MOM: I finally got it right.

Firsts

DAD: Love you

ME: OMG did you just send a text??

DAD: Is that what i did?

Distortion

MOM: You hurted my feelings {:>(.

ME: Why do you have such a large nose? and a unibrow?

MOM: The sadness has distorted my facial features.

Emotional

DAD: Ill see u later :-) =D ;)

ME: Did you actually just use emoticons?

DAD: Im really emotional

Largish File

MOM: Beloved family. PLEASE DO NOT CALL ME i am downloading a largish file n need to not be interrupted. S/b done by 8:15 or so. Thank you!

Glasses Needed

ME: My suitemates scare me

MOM: What's a suiternate

Old School Recipe

DAD: Get some pepto-bismol from CVS & some soups of your choice. Mom made soft rice & steamed neocolonialism.

DAD: Broccoli

Dr. Gul

DAD: dont forget you have the dentist next week

ME: ok

DAD: hes new, his name is Dr. Gul

DAD: Dr Gul

DAD: Dr Gul

DAD: Dr GUL

DAD: Gul

ME: OK I KNOW HIS NAME

Intercepted

ME: Dad, can you send me your credit card number so i can put more money onto my food account?

DAD: Will call. Dont want to get intercepted.

That Helps

MOM: You left your phone on the counter!!!!!!

Texting?

DAD: Is this a text?

ME: No its an email

DAD: but I sent it from my cellphone...

MASTER CLASS

Lauren: At first Marti Schmidt Kaelin struggled with texting. The very first texts on the website (see "The Origin Story," page 1) reflect the frequent misspellings and grammatical challenges that she faced in those early days—*Doyle* not *Boyle* (see page 20).

Now Marti falls into a new stratum of texter: Master Class (see "Mobile Mouse," page 142).

Marti has embraced her Internet celebrity and taken the challenge to perfect her craft seriously. She now corrects misspellings and insists on the relevancy of the new format. "It's the perfect way to get in touch with your children."

The other day, Marti tried to teach my father how to text.

"Click on Messages, Mark, then just type. You can even insert a picture. It's easy."

Oh, how far Marti—and the parents in these texts—have come.

Blam!

DAD: By the way, my new nickname is fre$h money Mike. or F'dub. The reason I use the ke$ha thing is two fold: it's a money symbol but also because… wait for it…." the party don't start 'till I walk in." Blam!

Ready

MOM: my phone has texting now!

ME: welcome to 2011. :)

MOM: my glasses are ready at hand

Happy Uterus

MOM: how do you feel?

ME: awful. my uterus hates me.

MOM: but your not pregnant so it doesnt hate you this month

MOM: (\:D/) <– happy uterus

Midterm Angel

ME: Wish me luck! About to take my midterm!

MOM:)8(

MOM: I sent an angel to watch over you!

:-)3

MOM: :-)3 Dimple chin man

Bowtie Man

MOM: Can you please call me when you need to be picked up! Don't do anything stupid! :-)8

ME: What is that emoticon?

MOM: bowtie man! He doesn't do anything stupid*

*"Bowtie Man" was submitted anonymously, and it is still one of the funniest texts to date. When we doubt the longevity of our website, or its hilarity, there is always Bowtie Man. He doesn't do anything stupid.

Money

ME: Hey mom can you transfer some money over for me

MOM: Does it look like I have ...(_$_)

ME: What is that supposed to be?

MOM: Does it look like I have money coming out of my ass?!

Missing Persons Report

MOM: Amber Alert! Missing 22 yr old. Brown hair blue eyes 5'3" app 116 lbs. Last seen with boyfriend. Believed he took her to his residence. If you find her send her home. Her mother misses her. $10.00 reward.

Breathe Right

ME: it's okay i'll call in a bit

MOM: K. :z) that's a smiley with a breathe-right strip! Haha

Froggie

ME: I GOT THE JOB!!!!

DAD: YAY! @_____@!!!! (Froggie's happy too!)

ME: ....really, Dad? Froggie?

Waxing Poetic

DAD: A crisp autumn breeze rustles through the colorful trees of Maryland on a sunny November day, beckoning you home.

Mom's Morning Report

MOM: Be careful driving to work tomorrow. Fog in the A.M. This message brought to you by mom.

ME: Thanks.

MOM: I was gonna say "this messsage brought to you by moms. We worry so you don't have to."

A Cheerleader

MOM: I am so incredibly proud of you! *\O/*

ME: Thanks mama. What the hell is that symbol thing? A clown nose getting squished between two magic wands?

MOM: It is a CHEERLEADER . . .

BBM "Read"

MOM: U wake???????????? :)

MOM: I know u read it :) :) :) :) :)

Boobs

MOM: :)B OLD

MOM: :)8 YOUNG

Whereabouts

MOM: Just wondering as to your whereabouts…please check one of the following boxes.
___dead in a ditch
___alive in a ditch with broken fingers
___jail
___Mars
Thanks, your roommates

Tactics

DAD: sorry i missed your call. call me back when U have time.

ME: i didn't call you…

DAD: I know, that's my new tactic! It worked how are you whats going on?

Chubies

DAD: Yo what up chubies…. thats how t9 spells bitches

Pile

MOM: hi

ME: hi

MOM: ~@~

ME: is that a pile of shit?

MOM: yup

Monkey Face

MOM: @(*.*)@

ME: ???

MOM: its a monkey lol

Being Cool

DAD: mt dishwasher!

ME: Mount Dishwasher?

DAD: No, empty dishwasher, I was being cool.

Goatee

DAD: : {)-

ME: What's that??

DAD: Smile with mustache and under lip hair

(o Y o)

MOM: Can you bring my sweater from the car? xx

ME: How cold is it? Should I bring mine too?

MOM: (o Y o) –> (. Y .)

Cyberhug

MOM: Night. BED time. Soooooo proud of you!

ME: K night

MOM: Sending cyberhug

MOM: (((((((john)))))))))

3<]

ME: Can you transfer more money? I need a plane home. xx love you

DAD: 3<]

ME: huh? yes?

DAD: It is my foot in your ass.

Foursquare Champ

DAD: The good news is that I am just two days away from regaining my title as Mayor of Panera Bread...as long as that little bitch Matt keeps his skanky ass out of here.*

*Foursquare is an application for smartphones that claims to be a virtual exploration tool. You can sign in at various locations and keep tabs on your friends. If you frequent an establishment, Foursquare gives you badges: Newbie, Explorer, Adventurer, etc. If you frequent an establishment enough—for instance, Panera—Foursquare can give you the esteemed title of Mayor. If there's one parent we'd really like to meet, it's this dad.

Efficiency

DAD: mom fell. broke her jaw. four stitches. she's fine.

ME: she okay?! was this a mass text!?

DAD: yes. and yes, it was most efficient that way.

Proud

ME: Got accepted to OU

DAD: O U did?

DAD: Congratulations!

DAD: Fwd: O U did? Get it?

Cats and Dogs

ME: Its raining cats and dogs out there.

DAD: I know i just stepped in a poodle.

:/)

MOM: U should stop for gas at Hess in Clinton - cute gas girl :/)

ME: What's the face?

MOM: Happy penguin :/)

Rabbit

MOM: We r in costco. Ur dad is annoying I made u a rabbit. Eat Well sleep well. love mom
(_(\
(=' :')
(,(")(")

Mime

DAD:

ME: blank message?

DAD:

ME: …?

DAD: Im a phone mime ! :)

Swiped

DAD: my new phone has swiping instead of texting! swiped.

ME: that's so cool dad!

DAD: i know! swiped

ME: ….why do you keep saying swiped?

DAD: to let you know i'm swiping..not swiped.

A-

ME: Mom, I got an A- on my test!

MOM: Not an A?

ME: No… That's good stop.

MOM: FYL. Like FML but you.

Beep

ME: Is it raining there?

DAD: ? I am leaveing now

ME: Okay beep your horn when you get here.

DAD: Beep

ME: Dad really?

5½

MOM: Those bball shorts for $6 (regular $20) which is so cheap to begin with. Are 5½ phone lengths long. Is that to short for you?

Evil Bowtie Man

MOM: ;->8

ME: Is that an evil bowtie man?!?!

MOM: Bowtie man cant be evil because being evil is stupid & he never does anything stupid.

Leggings are not pants.

DAD: in baltimore airport again…all i have to say is L.A.N.P.!!!!!!!

Ice Spiders

ME: Do you know that you have an automatic signature? After every text you send this appears:)o(

DAD: That's an ice spider*

*Intrigued by this text, we did some research on these elusive creatures. To the best of our knowledge, they do not exist except for in a 2007 made-for-TV movie, Ice Spiders, featuring Vanessa A. Williams (not the famous one).

WHEN GRANDPARENTS TEXT

Sophia: My grandmother (or as I like to call her, Gigi) just turned ninety. When I first told her about *When Parents Text,* she was immediately proud of me, even though I don't think she fully understood what I was doing. "I always knew Sophia was going to do something special," she told my mom.

From that moment on, she became the number-one fan of the site. She once called me and recited over twenty messages she found particularly hilarious. Though she has not mastered the art of text messaging just yet, she always seems to get a kick out of the small portion of *When Parents Text* that is dedicated to her generation.

"How did they learn how to text?" she asked me. "Those keys are so hard to press!"

iTunes

GRANDMA: U need to come back 2 my house and unalphabetize my music. I do NOT listen 2 it that way…

FB

GRANDMA: can you help me sometme this week with making a profile pictute on FAcebook?

ME: yes but i wont be home until 7:30 this whole week.

GRANDMA: i dont really wear jewlery maybe some pajamas if u see any that look cute with liHi how are you?

Boom Box

GRANDMA: I dont know how to make dinner more festive we need music I'll see if I can borrow a boom box but you'll have to bring the disks

Hi

GRANDMA: Hi.

ME: Hi! Have you learned how to text?

GRANDMA: This is grandma

ME: Are you enjoying your visit?

GRANDMA: Yes bye

Pandora

GRANDMA: Please help - after a while, Pandora stops playing. It says, "Are you still listening? We don't want to play to an empty room." The room is not empty - where does it think i went. I want it to keep playing. Help.

Creepy

GRANDMA: Hey Haley B. Please let's get together soon. I miss you and I want to smell your hair.

Skyping

GRANDPA: Hey Jillybean, does the computer have to be on for meto skype?

Placement

GRANDMA: 11 -@# %&**()+-¿/=( ) <> / <>;'"".com.com @ @@c'@ @!?!?..m

(five minutes later)

GRANDMA: DISREGARD MESSAGE. was checking new symbol placement.:)

Dotted

GRANDMA: H.e.l.l.o.h.o.n.e.y.t.h.i.s.i.s.m.y.f.i.r .s.t.m.e.s.s.a.g.e.i.m.i.s.s.y.o.u.a.m.e.

Rowdy Grandma

GRANDMA: Hi have you tried that whipped cream with alcohol?

All My Plans

GRANDMA: hi- all my plans are changed. james can go home so i am on my way to get him. he wants to go home so thats where i am taking him then will go see mom after. had to stop and get his clothes fr paula. she was totally busy with lunch so i am getting a mini pizza at the hut next door. i can eat it in the car. i looked at my face when i was getting ready. used the magnifying mirror today. i had hair growing from my eyebrows to my lids….gross. please tell me in the future if i have a lot of hair growing where it shouldnt be. keep in mind that i cant see well anymore. thanks. -hairy grama!

Killin It

ME: Have to work til 10. Have fun with Janet!

GRANDMA: On the patio killin a pitcher of margaritas. Thank u for teaching me!

No Punctuation Needed

GRANDMA: Do u plan to do college interview with college person making strawberry shortcake friends coming for overnite what do i do when my computer is fuzzy gramps is trying to figure it out takes forever help me whats new? love, me

Hyperabbreviation

GRANDPA: Hey Sweety (or is it Sweetie - android prefers ie) Srry I missed u. We're freezg up here in NY xcpt ystrdy-flt lik sprng! Hows cllg life? Hows ur apt+ur rmm8? ML, Gpa

Many Words

GRANDPA: Did you get done at school just wondering. Did you move back home. Your mom did not say when she talked to gramma. How about all these words in one text. Just patting myself on the back ha ha.

Computer Magic

GRANDMA: I spoke into the computer and nothing happened

Grandma's Butt

GRANDMA: "HEY girl. How is Prince Charmong. Lov U with all my Butt. I would say "heart" but my Butt is bigger. LOL."

The Lovely Bones

GRANDMA: Omg, I'm watching this movie called "The Lovely Bones" and the little brother in the movie has that same Mexican puppet we have that freaks u out.

Eagle

GRANDMA: Eagle just flew across deck i was out there he says hi

WORLD WIDE WEB

Sophia: When we first got Internet in our house, my mom taught me how to create an e-mail address and sign in to AOL. I can still remember the annoying dial tone and the yellow man dashing across three pictures.

My parents knew little about the Internet, and I knew even less. They used it as a way to connect with family members and people they worked with. I used it to talk to all of my friends in my sixth-grade class.

Over the years, my friends and I began to connect to the Internet for entertainment. Napster, YouTube, LiveJournal, Myspace, and Facebook became important websites for everyone I knew. We used it as a way to communicate, to translate our French homework, and to blog about our every thought.

When my mom finally got on Facebook two years ago, I taught her how to sign in to her account and write on someone's wall. We had come full circle.

Information Highway

DAD: Dear son, with new toy in hand and text messaging for the first time, I enter the 21st century, no longer roadkill on the super-information highway. I know not what path I follow but I am resolute to the task. For in the words of the inimitable Yogi Berra, "If you don't know where ur going, u might end up somewhere else."

love dad

Google Earth

MOM: Are you at home now?

ME: Yeah. Why?

MOM: I'm on google earth and looking at your house. Wave at me through the window!

Old, Stinky, and Bald

DAD: OMG just hooked up wii to the internet and signed up for netflix - I may never leave my chair again

ME: haha that's awesome! I love netflix!

DAD: No seriously you will fine me old, stinky, and bald some day just sitting here watching a movie

The Best

MOM: Your profile picture is the greatest! Yes one of the best. I love it. That's why I love facebook. That's why I'm on. You guys are the best. I love being a part of it all. And I can go from one kid to another. Yes it is the best*

Chirping

MOM: chirp chirp…that's me tweeting. Lol

*This mom *is* the best.

Unamused

MOM: Can you block your list of friends from non-Facebook friends? It's too personal.

ME: No, sorry.

MOM: (?_?) unamused face

Password I

MOM: my username is rockinout and the password is chocolate

Password II

ME: Whats your computer password?

MOM: bubbles

Password III

ME: I need your e-mail password

MOM: HOTMOM (in big letters)

Password IV

MOM: I'm not making this up-if anyone ever asks u why u are so weird there is an example- dad protected his profile on his computer and I needed something to I managed to pry the password out of him- it is f*ck

Pal O'Mine

DAD: I just saw on tv that 73 percent of kids on facebook have their parents on their buddy list

DAD: How bout it pal o mine?

Confirming

DAD: Quick ? How do you accept a friend request?

ME: press confirm

DAD: I know, but after that

VCR

DAD: Do you have a VCR? You know, so we can Skype later?

Robbed

MOM: Please dont mention on facebook or to your friends we are gone. Do not want to get robbed. Xoxo

Upside Down

MOM: Is it bad that it took me 10 minutes to open my laptop because i was trying from the wrong side? The apple was upside down!

The Judds

MOM: Hi honey, be proud. Was watching Oprah and wanted to know a name of a guest so I googled 'big fat Judd sister'. The first answer was her. Have a good day!

"Available"

MOM: I think I just changed my status, what does it say?

ME: It doesn't say anything.

MOM: I prefer to say nothing. Why does dads say available. Doesn't mine also?

MOM: Do I have to type in available? I thought it was automatic

ME: Mom no.

MOM: Look now

ME: It doesn't stay anything.

MOM: So strange. I just typed it in edit my profile

ME: Ok your status says available now but mom that's weird.

MOM: Yes it's all good now. Moving on!

Social Dating Sites

MOM: I was browsing the inet for social dating sites (for your sister but don't tell her, thanks) and came across this neat site. It's called Face Book. Just type it into google search. It will pop up.

Norbet and Daggett

ME: Did you know Angry Beavers is on Netflix? Instant!

MOM: SHUT UP!!!

Caps Lock

MOM: i want to show you a video online, but the password isn't working

ME: is it on caps lock?

MOM: no it's on youtube

Online Videos

DAD: This video I was watching online, it went what people call "viral". Have you heard that word? Viral?

Facebook Chat

MOM: one of ypor friends facebook chatted me. Do I respond. If yes, what do I say? Pleaz help. Come home NOW.

(five minutes later)

MOM: Do you think this is funny??? COME HOME NOW, I am really feeling thr pressure! Help your mother!

Skype

ME: Why did you sign off on me?

MOM: Had to poop

Relationship Status

MOM: Who are you in a relationship with?

ME: What?

MOM: Your facebook page says that you're in a relationship!

ME: How would you know that?

MOM: Becca has facebook and she told Zinny and Zinny called daddy and daddy called me.

MOM: Who are you in a relationship with?

Frowny Face

MOM: I had 70 friends. Now, I have 69. Frowny face...and I don't even know who is missing, but it makes me sad.

Hashtag Humor

MOM: I made a tweet! I used a pound sign and everything just like u do!

Jewel Quest Demo

MOM: $28 charge on my bill 4 CASUAL DATA USAGE.

ME: That's the internet, ma. I told you not to go there without a plan.

MOM: You don't think I'm using it playing the Jewel Quest demo do you? 957 THAT'S A LOT OF MINUTES. It's the only thing I can think of!

Chicken Parm Tonight

MOM: I'm on twitter now. I tweet all day!

MOM: ooo laaa laaa, JLO is making chicken parm tonight. mmmm

ME: I hope this is a joke.

MOM: twitter me! everyone is following me everywhere

Noodle About

MOM: What's that site you like to find jokes on? Noodle About?

ME: Stumble Upon.

Dirtbag

ME: Yeah i sent him a facebook message and he didn't respond

MOM: when did you send it?

ME: Yesterday

MOM: Dirtbag

Twitter Friends

MOM: I didn't know you had the twitter! Me too! I'm only friends with Elisabeth Hasselbeck and Pioneer Woman. Want to be friends? (:

At Desk Studying

MOM: i just stalked your facebook. could you post just ONE picture of you at a desk studying?

ME: hahahah very funny mom!

MOM: no really and both you and your sister should cover up leave some room for the imagination

Googling

ME: Hey, check out whenparentstext.com

MOM: funny they should also make a website for "when eight year olds use google"

MOM: some of Sammy's latest googles include "are mermaids evil" and "how to make a real baby dinosaur"…

Number One Search Engine

ME: Dad, I have had this bruise for 3 weeks and it is still huge! Should I be worried?

DAD: Yes.

ME: Well idk what to do!

DAD: Ask Jeeves

ME: That's not funny. What do I do?

DAD: I wasn't trying to make a joke. Ive heard you can ask them anything.

FFF: Facebook Friends Forever

MOM: I promise I will always be your facebook friend.

Postcollege Options

DAD: Maybe you can work for the IRS. (if you don't know what that is, look it up on facebook or something like that)

Surfing

MOM: i think i just kicked myself out of facebook

ME: hahahahaha how??

MOM: surfing the net.

Popular

MOM: Women having buttocks enhancements. Round bottom popular says Internet

Church Updates

DAD: So how was your homily?*

ME: It was okay. He just kind of repeated the gospel.

DAD: Ours was about Internet Porn.

*For the nongentile, a homily is a commentary that follows a reading of scripture during Mass.

Royal Wedding

MOM: Don't google search anything about the royal wedding. On the news they said it will be a superbowl for viruses. The first 22 sites google for "royal wedding dress" were infected. Also, could I get u to email me those pics on ur camera please :-)

Harmony

DAD: Does anybody know Harmony? She wants to be friends with me on Facebook. She may be one of these internet floozies looking for a boyfriend and she needs to know I am too hot to handle for her.!!!!!!!!!! (Ran out of exclamation points)

iRoller

DAD: We saw Steve Wazniak -sp? On a segway rolling down the sidewalk in front of Safeway.

Face Page

DAD: Tell Rach that- it on her fp

ME: Fp?

DAD: Face page

ME: You mean facebook?

DAD: Ha ha. I'm so antiquated

Divorce

DAD: I'm not sure but I think I just accidentally divorced your mom on facebook... I'll keep you updated.

ME: (silence)

MOM: why is your father married to his sister on facebook?

Quidditch

DAD: twitter? thats the same thing as quidditch right?

Wrong Screen

DAD: Gibson recording king

DAD: Bret favored college

DAD: Sorry for the bizarre text's. Tried repeatedly to search the web from the wrong screen.

Rekindled*

MOM: Ken and Barbie are back together!!

ME: Did they break up?

MOM: Hellooooo in 2004, but they rekindled at toy story 3, and made it official on v-day, aren't you facebook friend with them?!

In 2011 Barbie and Ken released a statement stating, "We may be plastic, but our love is real." As of this writing, they were still together.

Respectfully

MOM: Dearest katie, I respectfully ask that you delete your last two facebook posts regarding being drunk and naked.

Love, mom

Pending

DAD: Had to pick up your sister, missed yoga tonight :-(

ME: Sorry I could have picked her up if I knew you had plans.

DAD: No probs…gives me time to check in on the 12 friend i have pending on Facebook.

OCCASIONS

Lauren: My mom recently found a dust-covered box in the basement that contained dozens of home movies—VHS tapes chronicling years of diligent soccer game, recital, and school play attendance. One of the videos was of a special performance that my mom recorded as a holiday message to my grandfather.

Close-up on my sister and me, eleven and six years old. My mom has dressed us in our best red floral dresses: bows, cap sleeves, and lace with thick black tights. Zoom out. We are standing on a staircase, the banister wrapped with a holiday garland covered with fake poinsettias and plastic beads. My mother's voice off-camera: "Go!" We excitedly burst into the worst version of "Santa Claus Is Coming to Town" you can imagine.

It's clear that my sister tried to teach me a sequence of hand motions to coincide with the lyrics. *Making a list, checkin' it twice, gonna find out who's naughty and nice.* "Pretend you're holding a list, look it up and down, then point to either side of the room." As we sing, we try to walk synchronized down the stairs. Halfway through the song, I forget what I'm doing and look to my sister for guidance. Her eyes have not wavered from the camcorder. She's got the hand motions down.

Scene change. We're off the stairs now, and the music has changed to an instrumental number. My sister and I are doing an interpretative dance to "Carol of the Bells," spinning in wide circles and doing dramatic leaps in our entryway.

Let's be thankful that today you can just send a holiday text message.

Happy New Year

MOM:

Drinking and Driving

MOM: Don't Drink and Drive!!!!!!!!

MOM: Don't Drink and Drive

MOM: Don't Drink and Drive!!

MOM: Happy New Year!!!!!!!!!!!

MOM: Don't Drink and Drive

NYD

MOM: Happy hangover, sweetie. Be sure to clean up the bathroom. Love, mom.

Sound Judgment

MOM: HAPPY 2011. WE LOVE YOU!

MOM: Remember when parents text?? that's what I'm doing!

ME: Habjmmmm

MOM: What is that response? an inebriated laugh?

MOM: Where are you?

MOM: ???????

MOM: Do not get into a car of anyone was drinking the concoctions that were left around the kitchen They will be sick and have little evidence of sound judgment.

New Year's Eve

MOM: Eat before you drink and have a fat or oil or nuts. No Tylenol!! Hydrate!! Eat pizza before you go out, eat eggs in the AM! WATER BETWEEN DRINKS!!!! Nuprin before bed!! I love you, Mom!

February 13

MOM: Hey. This is from my new droid. :) what are you doing tomorrow for dinner?

ME: A droid!?! Very exciting! I have no plan for dinner. What about you?

MOM: Sending you valentine's pizza. Address?

Valentine's Day

DAD: Happy Valentine's Day! Love, baba

ME: You too! Except mine is filled with class and homework and no chocolate!

DAD: I can chocolate you. Tell me what tickles your fancy.

Broken Heart

DAD: Mom broke our wedding picture. Happy Valentine's day.

V-Day Fartbus

ME: Dad, I'm sad I'm alone. Also, the bus smells like farts.

DAD: There's a great guy right now on a fartbus thinking there's never gonna be a nice girl who appreciates me.

Worst Ever

DAD: McRibs are gone! Worst Valentine's Day ever!

St. Patrick

MOM: +<|:-|~~ (St. PATRICK chasing the snakes out of Ireland. Happy St. Patty's to ya!

Modern Times

MOM: can we skype you into the seder tonight?

Ash Wednesday

MOM: hey know what? I love you thats what!!

ME: i'm so glad to hear that

MOM: I'm glad you're glad +:) (that's an Ash-Wednesday-is-coming-soon smile face- get it? See, she's got a cross of ashes on her forehead!)

Daylight Savings

MOM: Don't forget about your cocks tonight

Grilled Cheese

MOM: Just heard on the news that today is national grilled cheese day - hope u celebrated properly

ME: I had no idea! I already ate dinner, oh well maybe next year

MOM: I'll make a note on the calendar

Two Holidays

MOM: I dont get some of the things on this when parents text website

ME: Like what?

MOM: 4/20?? ({})?

ME: National Marijuana Day and a vagina

MOM: Ahhh I had my suspicions... Hardboiling eggs for Easter!

Easter Bunny

MOM: Hello Kathleen!!! What would you like in your easter basket??? You've been a very good girl this year!!!! Heeheehee -The Easter Bunny :))))

Easter Eggs

DAD: i rly had to flatulate during easter dinner so i sat the tray of deviled eggs next to my plate to cover my tracks. genius i know.

ME: gross. i ate one of those.

DAD: added a little umpph to the flavoring im sure

Cinco de Mayo

ME: Where is everyone?

ME: Why are there empty beer bottles everywhere?

ME: Where is the dog?

MOM: cinc0 de mayo!!!1111

Costume Contest

DAD: For Halloween I am going to wear a t-shirt with "Fe" written on it. Who am I?

DP and Golfballs

DAD: I got tricker - treaters out the yang …
and we got no candy.

ME: Start handing out the cans of DP in the
fridge.

DAD: I.m given used golf balls. What.s dp?

Dad Gift Guide I

ME: any Christmas ideas for you?

DAD: hmmm. maybe a couple of ties, I tend
to like conservative boring ties. any kind of
munchies - cheese, peanuts, beer - always
good. maybe a new pair of gloves. Thanks for
asking. dunkin donuts gift card. ;)

Dad Gift Guide II

ME: Where's your Christmas list dad?

DAD: A map of Texas would b nice

Dad Gift Guide III

ME: Have you been thinking of gifts?

DAD: not too much. needed a new razor and bought that. we talked about a new tv for the bedroom and bought that. just something small, having you home is the best present i could get.

(three hours later)

DAD: i need a new car wash brush on a pole. get it when you get home.

Dad Gift Guide IV

ME: What do you want christmas dad?

DAD: Peace on earth good will to all.

ME: No. Really.

DAD: Fine. Boxer briefs... Calvin Klien or Puma Size 34

91

Dad Gift Guide V

ME: Hey, what do you want for Christmas?

DAD: remington 1187 premier shotgun

ME: LOL, k, what else?

DAD: hair

Dad Gift Guide VI

ME: what do you want for christmas, dad?!

(nine days later)

DAD: Coffee-starbucks,dark roast (Ethiopian, Guatemalan, or Latin American Blend); note cards (postcard size ONLY- with a nice border, thick stock (for MEN); reading glasses (3 pack if you can find it); 2.5 power Uniball pens-the pack from office max-vision needle, micropoint, paul shanklin CD-songs of the revolution (political satire) pties with patterns -i have enough solids- (you can get them at tjmaxx so you don't have to spend a lot of money)

Dad Gift Guide VII

ME: What do you want for Christmas?

DAD: Hi. We have a new cheese lasagna recipe. My list; Bananagram and .09 Pentel lead pencil. Love you.

Trader Joe's Turkey

MOM: Hey! I was just looking in the Trader Joe's flyer so, I guess you'll be having Tofurkey for Thanks giving! Tofobble, fobble!!! :)

Thanksgiving

MOM: Can you please tell the relatives you're pregnant so I don't accidentally say something? I'm afraid to speak.

Subtle Guilt Trip

MOM: we got the tree do u want to decorate on monday with everyone or should i do it? there is no right answer we all need to be honest

Hanukkah Commute

ME: Wires down at penn station, i'll take the bus back

MOM: Ok be careful!!!

ME: of what?

MOM: I don't know, it's windy!

ME: but i'm commuting underground...

MOM: that's true, HAPPY HANUKKAH!!!!

Ten

MOM: On a scale of 1 to 10 how much would you like to have a digital picture frame?

Camel

DAD: Put a new light in the camel so your friends would stop making fun of the nativity set on the lawn.

Jolly

MOM: Fuck santa. If I had a million little elves helping me and random people feeding me cookies, I'd be jolly all the time too.

Nativity

MOM: Can you go look for Joseph? A neighbor said he was missing.

Ornament Choices

MOM: Do u want a pickle that calls out hints to where hes hiding ornament or a reindeer with a grill with food on his butt for ur ornament?

HAPPY BIRTHDAY!

Who better to wish you happy birthday than the people who gave you life?

Twenty-Seven

MOM: Wow I wanted to be first. But I missed it 6am. Was too late. You are half my age today. 27 +27 = 54

ME: Well my bday in Australia started yesterday.

MOM: ok

(two hours later)

MOM: We r getting red velvet cream pie, from Maria calendars in your honor

(twenty minutes later)

MOM: They were out no pie in honor

Nineteen

DAD: Happy birthday baby!!

DAD: are you one

DAD: are you two

DAD: are you three

DAD: are you four

DAD: are you five

DAD: are you six

ME: oh please no.

DAD: are you seven

DAD: are you eight

DAD: are you nine

DAD: are you ten

DAD: . . .

DAD: . . .

ME: 19! yay good guess.

Balloons

MOM: Check your schedule and let me know whats better, which day? what time? if your bringing friends?how many?what you want to eat??????XOXO

ME: okay party planner

MOM: Oh I love that! I'm your party planner! :+) O O <-balloons

Bon Jovi

ME: mom what do you want for your birthday

MOM: A nice mat 2 stand on in front of the sink, a pretty hand soap dispenser or bon jovi in my cupboard

Twenty-First

DAD: mom says she told you to be careful, i say get drunk and puke. love you

Virtual Message

DAD: Please send your mother a virtual message for her birthday.

ME: Do you mean an e-mail?

DAD: Here is a sample "Happy Birthday Mom! Love, Angela"

Worth It

MOM: I absolutely must talk to you on your birthday, you must call me :-). Love mom... the woman who birthed you...with no pain meds...so your brain would be perfect and unaffected by drugs...it was painful...but worth it...please call...

Old Man

ME: Happy bday old man

DAD: This came to me by error. sorry, no old men here

5:23 A.M.

DAD: Call Sam, it's his birthday

DAD: I sent Sam a cake… Your name is on it.

DAD: Chocolate mouse.

DAD: Moose.

DAD: Mose

DAD: Muose

DAD: Fluffy creamy chocolate

DAD: Stuff

DAD: Did the snow melt?

Rectal

MOM: I remembered the other birthday gift you could get for your dad - a thermometer (rectal). I guess they don't go on sale until Christmas, so you could get him one then.

"Happy Birthday"

MOM: Hey! Check out the birthday greeting I put up on your brother's FB!

ME: Okay.

ME: It just says, "Happy birthday!"

MOM: Yeah. I thought it would be nice.

Only Twenty-Nine This Year

ME: HAPPY BIRTHDAY

DAD: Thank you!! Be home to celebrate my 29th tonight?? :)

ME: Hahahahahaha you wish

DAD: :)– (that's a beard below my smile). Grandma sent me $50 like she does every year– someone should explain price inflation to her. $50 doesn't go as far as it used to! (hint hint)

MEALTIMES

Lauren: On *Leave It to Beaver,* when Beaver runs out of the house, baseball glove in hand, mischief in his eyes, his mother shouts after him, "Be home for dinner!" It seems that little has changed since the 1950s sitcom. The submissions to our site suggest that grown children all over the world are receiving reminders about mealtimes.

When Parents Text began with a mealtime text.

To this day, my mother is rhapsodic over ground turkey. "Look," she'll say to me, grinning, pointing to the package of frozen meat, "Do you want tacos or meatloaf for dinner?"

I should be fending for myself—eating cereal for two meals a day and rationing rice portions. That isn't the case. My mother still cooks me dinner and reminds me to eat it. After four years apart, we fall back into these roles with ease.

"I'll have two tacos, please!"

Ribs for Dinner I

ME: When is my haircut?

MOM: Ribs for dinner

Ribs for Dinner II

MOM: I've just put my ribs in .I had another mammogram done and everything is ok.The ribs have nothing to do with it ,just that's what i'm having for dinner

Lag

MOM: We are having lag at maryanns and scotts

ME: Lag?

MOM: Lasagna

ME: You can't abbreviate lasagna

MOM: ok

Numbers for Dinner

ME: Hey mom what's for dinner?

MOM: We are having *7)80)*(*(980*)*(
(&89&(&987(&*&

Bribes

MOM: Come home!

MOM: We miss you

ME: I'm at the movies

MOM: We have Oreos

MOM: And milk

MOM: And fruit roll-ups

Perfection

ME: Whats for dinner?

DAD: Pasta with vodka sauce with bits of chicken sliced perfectly

Bacon Rage

ME: There's no bacon in the dining hall

DAD: Burn the place down

Put in Refrigerator

DAD: Get 20 pieces spicy chicken wings non breaded about 8.00$ they close at 10 pm put in refrigerator

DAD: Also get me metamucil sugar free

DAD: Also 2 gallon purified water

DAD: Also, get me greek salad and put it in the fridge

DAD: Never mind no greek salad

Sounding It Out

ME: Hi what's for dinner?

MOM: I'm thinking k-sa-di-a

Scraps

ME: Having dinner before we set off, we're all starving. You ok to grab something?

DAD: Yes. I'll find some scraps in the kitchen or eat with the cats. (or eat the cats)

ME: You're weird.

DAD: That's what hunger and loneliness does to you.

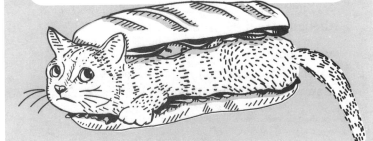

Pasta Recipes

MOM: Hi honey please stop using so much vodka for your pasta recipes we dont have any left XO mom*

Your child is drinking the vodka. See "Vodka Bottles" in the Diss section, page 247.

Pinot Grigio

MOM: i am at grandmas bring the pigno grisio.

ME: spell much?

MOM: thats not the issuw at hand.

Colon Blow

ME: just cooked a vegan dinner with alex! thought you'd be proud.

MOM: I am SO impressed! Sound DELISH! I just made a raw green soup in the Vitamix. Can you say "colon blow"?

Naked Pot

MOM: Naked Pot

ME: What?!

MOM: That was supposed to be baked potatoes! Mandarin salad

Cheesecake

MOM: You bring me a piece of white chocolate raspberry cheesecake and I will pretend we never had this conversation ;)

Bagels

ME: Dad, going to get bagels. Want anything?

DAD: Yes thank you.

ME: Eggs?

DAD: Eggs over easy onion bagel.

(one hour later)

DAD: Are you fucking serious?

Fast Food

MOM: Mexican stackup in 10 min. Snooz ya lose.

ME: I lost.

Sandwiches for Dinner

ME: Whats for dinner

DAD: sandwiches

(five minutes later)

DAD: who is this?

HAY

MOM: How was the kegger?!?

ME: it was good, now out to breakfast with some friends

MOM: hangover food HAYYYY

Breasts and Milk

DAD: Please bring home some (o)(o) & milk.

ME: ?

DAD: Doughnuts. :)

Invite

DAD: Do u want to come for dinner it just me and ham potatosalad

A1 for Waffles

MOM: Do you want waffles or muffins for breakfast? Just text "A1" for waffles or "B1" for muffins.

ME: Why did you go through all that trouble? Why can't I just text "waffles" or "muffins"?

MOM: We are texting in code! ;););) :)

ME: Waffles

MOM: A1 or B1?

ME: WAFFLES

MOM: Sooo…A1?

ME: Mom. Yes.

MOM: I think I would rather have muffins. I'm making muffins

Dumplings

MOM: Eating your leftover dumps and thinking of you! xoxo

ME: ....?

MOM: Remember how you ordered chinese food the other night? Well im finishing up the dumps.

Dinner Date

ME: Wanna do dinner or something this week? Monday maybe?

DAD: !!!! Ab so lu tely! Daddy love love love. Daddy love.

Secret Sandwich

DAD: can u bring me my sandwich into my room? Dont tell anyone i asked you this.

DAD: please, dont tell any one. please dont tell. Please dont say anything.

On Domino's Delivery Tracking

DAD: Jaun has double checked our order for perfection at 8:08pm! Good job Jaun! He sounds like a nice guy. The internet is a fascinating place.

Egg Salad

ME: what did you have for lunch?

DAD: Egg Salad. It smelled like a fart which was good. Afterwards I farted and it smelled like egg salad which was bad. Go Figure.

Twins

MOM: I just saw a heavy set older man in a velor track suit similar to mine @ cracker barrel. LOL!

OoOoOoOoO

DAD: Im making popcorn

ME: cool…save some for me!

DAD: nope

ME: ..why?

DAD: i already ate it. make your own popcorn. OoOoOoOoO

ME: wow thanks. and what are all those "o's" for?

DAD: their big and little popcorns. i bet no ones made that before!

Bagle n' Dirt

MOM: got u a bagle n' dirt cokr xo

ME: translation, mom? you got me a beagle and dirt?

MOM: sorry i was trying to text while driving. got u a bagel and a diet coke xo

Sushi for Dinner

ME: Sushi tonight?

DAD: Definitely

DAD: just you and me

DAD: ?

ME: K

DAD: You and me or the family.. or bring it home?

DAD: Make a decision…we can be together and talk

DAD: I would like that

DAD: Or we can go as a family which is good too.

DAD: You decide :-) there is no bad choice

ME: Stop texting me.

PETS

Growing up, neither of us had real pets in our household. Lauren had a bunny named Slipper, and Sophia had a goldfish named Skully. For this reason alone, we may never understand why almost 25 percent of our website is dedicated to the delicate relationship between parents and pets. Perhaps they are fillers for an empty nest, or maybe they've always been the family favorite. Either way, parents love to text about them, and we love reading the results.

Family Photo

MOM: can you be available about 1 PM on sunday for a family photo?

ME: Sure. Should I wear anything specific?

MOM: black, so the dog's colors will show best.

FWD

MOM: FWD: MEOW MEOW MEOW MEOW MEOW MEOW MEOW MEOW MEOW MEOW MEOW MEOW MEOW MEOW MEOW MEOW MEOW MEOW MEOW MEOW MEOW MEOW MEOW MEOW MEOW MEOW MEOW MEOW MEOW MEOW MEOW MEOW MEOW MEOW MEOW MEOW MEOW MEOW MEOW MEOW MEOW MEOW MEOW

Opposable Thumbs

DAD: The cat texted me, he wants to come in!! He's freezing in the bushes

Catnip

MOM: Hi Sweetie I'm getting Patches wasted

ME: How so?

MOM: Catnip. It's like pot

Goldie the Cat

MOM: Hi…it's goldie. i figured out how to use dad's phone. just wanted you to know i miss you. i was having a really good day with dad until i puked (i knew i shouldn't have eaten those plant leaves…) anyway, dad's kinda mad at me so i am hiding. can't wait to see you. your favorite cat, goldie

Trip to the Vet

MOM: it was a bite to the muscle, he's got a fever too, they took his virginity and butt temperatured him.

ME: wow mom, wow

Hail Mary

MOM: Pray for me. I am throwing up in the bathroom. Yuk! I need your prayers.

MOM: Surrounded by cats they don't know what to think.

Family

MOM: You will add the dog as your facebook friend RIGHT NOW!!

ME: mom he's a dog….

MOM: He is FAMILY, add him or you are grounded!!!!

Tinsel

MOM: Kitten just sneezed and i swore i heard a strange sound when i checked him ov i discovered tinsel in his nose when i pulled on it 12 inches came out-

Dog Days

MOM: the dog is in a mood today. ugh

MOM: Literally sniffing every blade of grass so gingerly. Been out here 20 minutes.

MOM: And now the dog is giving me the cold shoulder.

MOM: I love you!

Latest Accessory

MOM: Hey boo it's so cold i'm wearing the cats!

The Lord Giveth

MOM: big fish died today

ME: oh no! poor fish

MOM: the lord giveth and the lord taketh away, we now have 9 birds.

Monkey

DAD: Hi Monkey there is fleas in my house love dad

ME: What!? Seriously? Ah those stupid dogs shouldn't have gone inside.

DAD: Monkey yes I am agreeing I am upset going to panera love dad

Benadryl

ME: We're going to Jons

MOM: Hooray

MOM: The dog is so itchy. I gave him a benadryl

ME: what? why would you give a dog benadryl?

MOM: He's fucked up.

Patches

DAD: Can not make phils game tonite it is in san fran. I guess i will be watching at home with the only one who loves me. Thank you patches. By the way do u hv patches cell ph number or does he just use momas ph.

Squirts

ME: How was your day?

MOM: Kinda crazy…Amber woke up early (with the squirts) then there was a bomb threat at school so I was very late for work but other than that it was a nice day.

Cat Paw

DAD: Paw says Happy Wednesday. Wheres my tuna.

DREAMS

Why do people love to talk about their dreams?

Mass Text

MOM: Hi. I had a really weird dream. So let me ask you a weird question. Are any of you pregnant?

Wildest Dreams

MOM: Just saying in your wildest dreams what color kitchen aid mixer would you like?

MOM: False alarm. sorry. got excited at a macy's sale. please forgive.

Small Octopus

MOM: On my way, love you and great to see you, your room, your suitemates, your studio, and to do all the fun things! I must be feeling guilty about the cats because last night I dreamt that I had a (small) octopus and a horse that I had forgotten to feed. I really DID have a horse once, but I never had an octopus.

Happy Pride Month

ME: I had a dream last night you thought I was a lesbian haha!

MOM: It wasn't a dream

Battle

ME: I had a dream last night that we were dance battling. I can't remember but I think we tied.

DAD: Well, it was obviously a dream because I definitely would win the poppin and the lockin.

NO TATTOOS

ME: I had a dream last night that I got a tattoo. I started crying and freaking out in the dream because I knew you guys would be so angry. Luckily it washed off!

DAD: DON'T EVEN GET A DREAM TATOO!!!

Interpretations

MOM: I had a dream about rescuing a kitten last nite which I believe reflects my desire to be a grandmother someday

Someday

MOM: Someday i want to hold a penguin and rub its belly. It looks so soft.

Waist Deep

ME: We'll be in RI around 4:30 tomorrow

MOM: I had a dream last night that you were in a cave in waist deep water smoking pot.....

Haircut

MOM: I had a dream you got a dyke haircut.

Marshmallow Dreams

DAD: So I had a dream last night that I ate a huge marshmellow, and when I woke up my pillow was gone.

ME: Where was your pillow?

DAD: I don't know, I cant find it.

PIX

With the discontinuation of Kodachrome, our photographic dialogue is becoming more immediate, and mobile cameras have added a new texture to the way cell phone users communicate—"Aren't you jealous of where I am right now?" "Are these the socks you asked for?" "Look at this fabulous sandwich I am about to consume."

The modern postcard—picture messaging—is both versatile and humorous. When parents send picture messages, the possibilities are truly unbelievable, and the photo submissions that we have been saving for this print edition of *When Parents Text* have been some of the funniest to date.

Twenty-First-Century Parenting

MOM: I want a picture of u at her house.
either outside w house showing or w her
mom at home so i know ur there

Only in America

DAD: Only 2000

Birthday Is a Wash

DAD: happy birthday I hope you like what we got us for your birthday!

ME: what..........

Condom Cat

MOM: The cat wants to know why she found condoms in your laundry.

Gun Show

DAD: Funny face made from a white tail deer's butt LOL. At the gun show today.

My Naner

DAD: Sweetie sorry the visit was so short, I feel sad about that. I miss you.

DAD: this was sent from my new iphone by the way! Not my brick phone….

ME: Picture msg me then. If its not HD then you are lying. haha! love you!

DAD: I will as soon as I figure out how to do that???

Number One

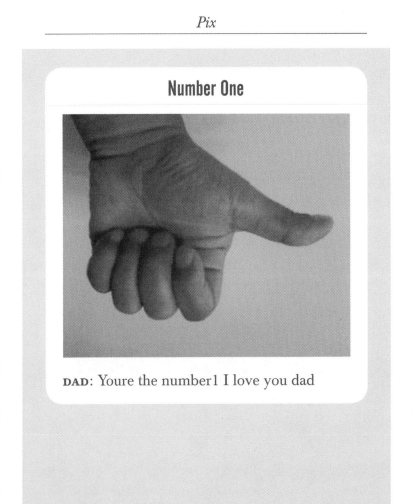

DAD: Youre the number1 I love you dad

Lost

ME: We're lost...can you send directions?

MOM: Sure.

(ten minutes later)

MOM: here is map

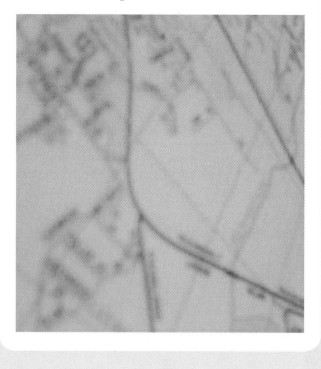

Regret

MOM: my greatest regret in life is that ill never have a dog

Mobile Mouse

MOM: Where is my mouse?

ME: I didn't move it

MOM: I saw it on booktable a few days ago; now I can't find it

ME: I didn't touch it

MOM: Why is it hanging with the snow people?

MOM: Didn't know it was mobile!

Stallion

MOM: New living room art

Do You Have a Clue?

MOM: Guess who?

Postcollege

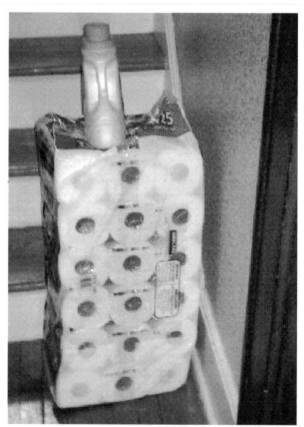

MOM: present! :)

Frankie's Fun Park

DAD: your grandmother wants to ride the motorcycle at Frankie's Fun Park. ONLY 3 TOKENS

ME: ...do what?

DAD:

WOW

There are some texts that you receive and immediately have to share. "Tacos for Dinner" was our first "wow" moment. From that day on we've received hundreds of messages that give us that same sense of astonishment.

Most of the time compiling the book was spent around the Kaelin dining room table, where we were served hot meals by Marti and laughed over thousands of messages. Most of the texts we went through could easily be grouped, but there were some that were too crazy and hilarious to fit into one category. Each and every one of these made us burst out laughing; all we could say was "wow."

Excursion Rules

DAD: Ok heres the skinny on our little excursion. All those riding with me meet at 2:00. Nick is taking the fun bus so its just you and your friends. Here are the ground rules everyone should bring a blanket and a pillow and give 25 dollars before we leave. Absolutely no contraban allowed. Code names or nick names are required on this trip. Mine is elvis, you will refer to me as elvis or sir only I will be treated with respect. I will have complete control over the radio and cd player. There will be singing. All fellow travelers will be required to sing along with at least one rolling stones song. Complaints about my singing or driving will not be tolerated, If these conditions are acceptable to you I will see you at 2:00.

Scheduling Conflicts

DAD: U know u r too busy when u have to schedule ur daily poop

(three hours later)

DAD: I write it in my planner as making a deposit at the bank so no one will know

Words with Friends

MOM: I am sitting at the orthodontist playing online scrabble with someone called Jesusboobs.

Inheritance

MOM: Hi boarding. If our plane goes down you get all my jewelry except the diamond ring that has a matching necklace and earrings. You get the necklace and earrings your brother gets the ring to use when he gets engaged :) He can get a different setting but he gets the diamond save this text

Potential

DAD: So, I found a new Mexican restaurant, very close to our house, for take out. Happy. On the way out, there's a machine with bouncy balls for only fifty cents. Very happy. A new house with hardwood floors to take the ball home to. Very, very happy. A high landing to drop the ball off onto a hardwood floor, Near ecstatic. Machine malfunctions and won't take my quarters. sad... Such potential.

Mucus

ME: I'm coughing up so much mucus. It's really gross.

DAD: Save it so i can analyze it i love mucus

Creative

MOM: I threw my Alfredo on the floor today sayin ayo there goes my lunch-o

Strange Sex

MOM: I just watched strange sex - new series girl has panic attacks in her vagina!

MOM: Its called vaginimus

Nectarines

DAD: THE NECTARINES ARE READY dont 4get. dad

DAD: I left a note on the kitchen table next to the bag of NECTARINES so u wouldnt 4get. its an orange note. he said that they would be ripe today so pls eat them. dad

DAD: did you see the note? it is orange dad

Hoot Hoot

ME: Did you make it back? How was your trip?

DAD: I SAW 41 OWLS ON THE WAY HOME. This is big. Huge.

Adrenaline

ME: YAY! The stuff we ordered is being delivered today

MOM: Woo Hoo – Ruth died, you know Uncle Lyman's wife, BUT I have your Braves tickets and check on the table!!

ME: Mom, that is the most insane text I've ever gotten

MOM: I know! My adrenaline is too high!!!!!!!!!!!

Circle of Life

MOM: I just witnessed the circle if life. I was watching some small birds out of our back window eating some birdseed from our feeder AND and a small vulture type bird flys in and carries off one of the small birds it was so sad - now no birds are coming around to eat

MOM: Do you want me to bring you a smoothie

Messed Up

MOM: Gotta take nap. Think axxidently took 2 tylemol pm instead of tyl cold. Gonna brief taje nap.

Too Much

MOM: Well just finished another episode of the Duggars. It's an old one though I've seen it before. It's the one where the mom WAS IN LITTLE ROCK TO STAY WITH THE NEW BABY AND THE FAMILY CAME TO VISIT. Sorry for all caps didn't want to delete. That woman is so crazy to have that many kids. NCIS is on next. It's a new one we haven't seen yet! It's only 10:00 so I'm sure you're not up yet. I cleaned out my purse and decided to change to the giraffe wallet. Think I may go to walmart later don't know what to make for your daddy for supper yet. Made pork chops last night but they were a little dry. Just filling you in no need to reply. Have a good day baby miss you luv u MOM

Feeling Better Now

ME: text me something to make me feel better! i need it!

MOM: thingamagingie that wibbles

MOM: there once was a man named John who had a big kabon

MOM: u need to talk?

MOM: want me to hold your beefstick and nuts?

MOM: success doesnt come to you you go to it.

Door Knockers

MOM: Hi Honey. If u find anything in Colonial Williamsburg that would be nice for the house such as a nice front door knocker call or text me

MOM: I am not interested in the pineapple door knockers

Doosie

MOM: Thats good, I knew I was going to have a doosie Monday when I cut my finger on the conditioner bottle in the shower and then there was a sand spur in my underwear.

Owl Homicide

MOM: How could anyone kick a owl? I find that very disturbing.

ME: …what? Aren't you driving?

MOM: No at work. Soccer player kicked a owl that was on the field. Owl went into shock and died :(

ME: #> owl with squished face

Third Time

DAD: tonight was the third time of my life that I did not immediately recognize you. Dad.

Kitchen Knives

DAD: I was showing your sister how sharp our new kitchen knives were and sliced my thumb open.

ME: Are you ok?

DAD: yeah I sewed in back together with some old sutures I had. I didn't have any numbing medication and had to push the needle through with a nail filer.

ME: oh.

Fly

ME: My roommate said she saw you today and that you looked super fly

DAD: Yep. I hope thats ok. to be fly

Bread Maker

MOM: Your dentist died. No appt next week. I'll find u new one. I learned how to make bread!!

Eagles

DAD: An otherwise dreary day, SAVED. Three male bald eagles are putting on a fantastic aerial show right outside my window overlooking the harbor. Floating, soaring, diving and hovering at heights low enough that one can almost count their feathers. Majestic and beautiful.

Phone Charms

MOM: My phone can hold charms!

ME: Nice. I take it you're looking for one, right now?

MOM: No, I'm just staring at it.

It Did?

MOM: I have a huge lasagna if you guys want to pick up bread

MOM: That sounded dirty

MOM: Sorry

Human?

MOM: Our church is going to be on the news tonight

ME: that's cool! what for?

MOM: A bone washed up in the ditch - They think it's human.

Peeing

MOM: Just got done peeing, pulling up my pants. I was going to see if u could bring me my bank card. Matt has it @ home. I'm hungry. That's ok I can run home.

Crappy Cruise

ME: How was your cruise?

MOM: Crappy cruise…old people really old. I was at teh 21 table and one woman died at the roulette. Guess her number was up.

½ to 40

DAD: Do you realize you are 37.5% done with college ?

DAD: …And I believe 20 years old is 1/2 to 40…And 1/3 of 60…

DAD: :D ?

Smokeless

ME: So if I told you I was going to the strip club when I came home, you would say?

DAD: Those are now smokeless. As are the dart places.

This is dad.

ME: Guess what I'm wearing

DAD: This is dad.

ME: ...yes. I'm wearing your sweater from the 80s.

Butter

MOM: Did you happen to put 6 sticks of butter in your purse before going to the mall?

ME: No

Drawing

MOM: I just drew the best strawberry ever.

Epic Song

MOM: what is the name of that song that is epic..that goes.. "dum dum DUM DUM (drums bum bum bum bum bum bum) dum dum DUM DUM" and then it is high notes and you feel like you can fly?

Oh, Not Much

MOM: 'Sup?

ME: Nothing, just made dinner. You?

MOM: bird died.

"Vagina"

MOM: When I came home from work today I was called Vagina from a little boy across the street who was on a scooter. He was with his sister and they both laughed. I turned around and said That's not nice Do you want me to tell your mother? They both said sorry

Dinner Party Guest List

MOM: O, forgot 2 mention others who will b @ dinner @ L's house, Jackie + kids, Carl + Melissa + her beau Igor (may b his son 2 who is H-school age + in football) L was in biz w/ Jackie in OH. Rich's sister in law, Dina (John, Rich's bro died of pancreatic cancer) + her newly widowed dad + Frank + one of her son's AJ (who, moved back from FRM New Zealand and worked in CO 4 a marijuana growing co. + is working on getting set up in that biz- huge $ in it.) Also, he has dreadlocks now!! He tiled the 1st house i had that was liquidated in my divorce. I think that's it, any ?s hehehe :)

Sweet

DAD: I just saw a horse scratching his neck on barbed wire.

ME: Sweet, Dad.

What Do You Need??

MOM: Are you near Barnes & Noble?

MOM: Or a IHOP? GOLDSTONE? CHILI'S? ETC. PLEASE ANSWER ASAP.

The Hawk

MOM: 40 to 50 mpr. winds snow tomorrow. the hawk is back.

ME: wow! winter! what's the hawk?

MOM: the cold winter blustery wind and snow. some people call it the hawk

Deposits

MOM: I just deposited love, hope, joy, health, & blessings in your account for 2011. Your pin is J.E.S.U.S. Please deposit

Breakfast Text

DAD: I need you to text me.

ME: ?

DAD: I'm bored. Sitting on the toilet waiting for the person next to me to leave so that I can release my bowels. What did you have for breakfast?

FANDANGO

DAD: If u ever get a chance try DENTYNE ICE ARCTIC CHILL ITS FANDANGO !!!

Circus

MOM: I'm getting read to watch some elephants eat and there is a juggler here with your juggling clubs

ME: Nice. Is he any good?

MOM: He was. The elephants are getting ready to eat watermelons.

War Story

MOM: so there I was doing a bug sweep before bed and a huge millipede was crawling behind the bed. It came toward me and I was screaming so Lu took off. Then it disappeared. So I thought I would go to bed. Then it was on the wall trying to attack. I screamed for your dad to come and kill it Long millipede later it was dead and had a funeral at sea.

ME: Long millipede later?

MOM: I was going to say to make long story short but then I wanted to work in long millipede

ME: Great story

MOM: the screaming was a bit over the top

Too Soon

DAD: Saki Bombing? The last time we put those two ideas together it was @ Pearl harbor? :P.

PLLLLLLLLL

DAD: I have ginger

ME: There is no need to text all three of us we are all together

DAD: PLLLLLLLLLLLLLLLLLLLLLL

ME: ?

DAD: Its the noise you make when you stick out you tounge and blow!!!

ME: This is going on whenparentstext.com

DAD: PLLLLLLLLLLLLLLL!!!!!

DAD: And dont forget, if it wasn't for me you wouldn't have a phone to use for texting :)

ME: You could have just said =P

DAD: Idk that one

Exercise

MOM: I started 2 do jumping jacks without my bra & almost knocked myself unconscious

Owl Call

MOM: Hi Hon! Miss u. Was thinking about when you ended up with two golden retrievers in the fancy museum covered in mud after you had just gone to your math tutor who taught you nothing! also just heard the coolest owl call… whheew wuwuwwu whooo whuu whooooooo

Yo-yo

DAD: I was a Yo Yo champion once

DAD: In the bronx

Cute

ME: Why do you still have this tiny jelly jar?

DAD: It's too small to keep nails and screws in.

ME: Ok…

DAD: But it is too cute to throw away!!!

Pelicans

DAD: Lake Whitney is covered with pelicans.

ME: That's great, but you do know that now 50% of your all-time texts to me are about pelicans.

DAD: And? I like pelicans. 66%

Wind Catchers

DAD: Your brother has reconnected with his hippie girlfriend. They have been here since last night. You could also call the show Birds of a Feather. She actually is real nice and seems to mellowed him a bit.

DAD: They make jewelry and wind catchers together. They have made some pretty cool stuff.

Toilet Problems

ME: Dad is driving me crazy with the toilet. I'm having them come fix it first thing in the morning. It's not a big deal. I don't see why he is flipping out.

MOM: Bcuz bathrooms r very important 2 him

Fuzzy

DAD: We played apples to apples and the word was fuzzy so I put down Fuzz and your brother put down fur - mom picked fur wtf

DAD: It cost me the game

Hot Commodity

MOM: Geezer following me around store bc i stopped to tie shoe and i guess he thought i was picking him up and another one in pking lot. Both decrepit. Tell your father to keep living.

VPL*

MOM: Well this should make u laugh and give u some new material…I finally bought some new underwear so now u cant see my underwear outline in my pants

ME: So necessary

TMI

ME: Have you left yet?

MOM: Dad found a nest of five baby rats in the garden and had to kill them with a shovel, gross. just leaving now.

Lost in the Supermarket

DAD: I lost your mom in the store.

(one hour later)

DAD: I wish she was taller, then I could find her.

*Visible panty line.

Parking Problems

MOM: Umm someone wrote something a very mean thing in the dirt on my car……..

MOM: It says. Learn to park

MOM: :'(

Super Mom

MOM: Just got an Amber Alert text. Be on the lookout for a 1998 Red Ford Taurus, license place DXM 284.

ME: Why do you get those things?

MOM: So I can help fight crime! I'm one of the good guys!

Big Poppa

DAD: I need a store that's just called "Fat Guy"….nothing fits me :(

Do It Up

MOM: did i tell you i'm going to florida this weekend?

ME: cool with who?

MOM: its going to be great...you know how i do it up...on the beaches..!

Re: Mom

DAD: Shes being menopausal im just rollin with it

Ladder

MOM: Won't be able to make it to your concert. Dad fell off the ladder.

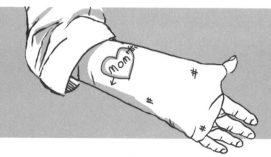

This Day in History

MOM: Crazy but true...Today in 1968 I got my period for the first time. Lol swear.

ME: hahahaha

MOM: For real! I remember cause I was at JFK going to grandma sally.

Razor

DAD: going to the hospital. razor scooter accident.

ME: weren't you going to work?

DAD: i ride my scooter to work

Collateral Damage

DAD: Fat woman fell on mom and pulled a muscle

When Parents Text Each Other: Costco

DAD: Got new card and I'm primary card holder.

MOM: Oh ok

MOM: Get low sodium soy sauce and vingar for our marindades

DAD: 300 12oz. cups for only $9.99! I was paying $2.50 for 50.

DAD: 152 gallon ziplocks for 9.99

DAD: They only half regular soy sauce.

DAD: I want to still use regular soy sauce

DAD: In line

DAD: Probably $175 total. I want to come back for six pack of PUR filters only $45

DAD: They sell caskets.

Camera Ready

MOM: is the camera ready?cause my face is.

Mustache

ME: Karina says you have a pretty epic mustache.

DAD: Its called beowulf.

It Could Happen

MOM: I took a new sleeping pill tonight. It says i may drive, eat, or have sex without knowing it.

ME: Uhhh...

MOM: Night!

Deer I Fear

DAD: hunting in tree.. luv u lots

ME: have fun

DAD: dont txt me bck idiot!!!! DEER r NEAR I FEAR.. turning fone off

ENTERTAINMENT

Sophia: My mom owns every season of *Mad Men.* Not to mention a themed hat and calendar. We're a family that loves entertainment. Though most of our days are spent out of the house, we always find time at night to catch up on our DVR and watch reruns of *Seinfeld.*

Unfortunately, while I was away at college, our yearly ritual of watching the Oscars had to be altered. Instead of making a bag of popcorn, betting on our favorites, and picking our own best dressed, our exchanges were limited to texting.

"Oh my god, look at how sexy John Hamm looks in his suit, with his beard!" was just one of the many gems I got from my mother on Oscar night.

Though this year we got to watch together again, I somehow missed the little one-liner messages sent to my inbox after every winner was announced.

Oprah

MOM: I watch Oprah, I feel like noting is impossible.

The K Drug

ME: Are you watching the game?

DAD: Saw a little. Are you watching it? Mom says to take your temperature!

ME: What my temperature???

DAD: Wooohooo! 41 to 26

ME: Haha. Why did mom say that?

DAD: She thinks you might be sick if you are watching Celtics. She wants meto watch Kardashians. NFW!!!

ME: Haha. Do it! So funny! Tell her it's what I do to go to sleep. Unlimited on netflix!!!!!

DAD: OMG. The K drug. They should use it for anesthesia.

Radio Disney

DAD: My life is over- they took ESPN sports radio off the air and replaced it with RADIO DISNEY. Feels like hannah montana stabbed me thru the heart with a mickey mouse pearl handles dagger

The Situation

ME: I am currently in the presence of some of the Jersey Shore cast members.

MOM: ARE YOU IN JAIL???

Wanted to Share

MOM: Turn on A&E

ME: I can't. I'm not at home. What's on?

MOM: It was a show about morbidly obese people and I wanted to share it with you

Yoda

ME: can you pick me up around 2 at school?

DAD: yeah, where?

ME: At school!

DAD: Yoda is my hero. He is your hero. He should be everyone's hero. He is the symbol of positive thinking. Be safe and may the force be with you. See you at two. Love daddy

Jeggings

ME: please look at the website whenparentstext.com

MOM: dad went to look. he says he doesn't get it

ME: hahahahah are you serious? What don't you get

MOM: Turn on conan. He's wearing jeggings.

Miley

MOM: I wanna buy a new cd. Recommendation off of the top of your head?

(two minutes later)

MOM: You're not fast enough. Bought Miley Cyrus. She can't be tamed.

Serious Discussion

MOM: are u free

ME: i'm at work i don't have any cell service

MOM: it's about lil wayne

Unstoppable

DAD: Lady GaGa is unstoppable.

ME: You know who Lady GaGa is?

DAD: Top of the charts in two weeks

Wolves I

MOM: come home and let's watch that movie where the wolves attack?

ME: I think you mean eclipse

ME: and…..no.

The Worst

DAD: Fucking Carrot Top is here

Wolves II

DAD: eclipse just got here. do u want me 2 save it 4 u?

ME: why are you watching that?

DAD: the wolves remind me of our dogs

JB

MOM: We R kewl parents now

ME: haha why?

(one hour later)

ME: mom where are you and dad?

(one hour later)

MOM: JB is so hot.

ME: Justin Beiber?

MOM: James Blunt.

MOM: Went to Boston and saw James Blunt at the House Of Blues. Your parents are so BA (bad ass) hehehe

Products

DAD: I wish queer eye for the straight guy would come back on. now i dont know what products to use on my face. oh mom wants you to pick up maple syrup

28 Days Later

MOM: Just watched 28 Days Later. I liked when they went to the Fresh and Easy market, but NOT when the dad got infected.

Crisis

MOM: Daddy just cancelled HBO what did you do to him this we

MOM: He. Also cancelled Showtime

ME: Why?

MOM: Text him He is cancelling everything!!!!

ALEJANDRO

DAD: Eleganté, eleganté!

ME: What the hell is that?

DAD: You know! That girl. Lady Gaga!

ME: . . . ALEJANDRO.

Discovery

MOM: Are you watching tv?

ME: No, why?

MOM: There's a great show on discovery fit and health

ME: What is it?

MOM: It's called my teens a nightmare, I'm moving out

ME: ....

MOM: I'm taking notes

Life Is Hard

MOM: Ok i have a big problem. You think u have it so bad. Wait until i tell u mine.. ok your dad is going to change back to dish network tomorrow n that means i have to watch two weeks of soap operas tonight before they get erased tomorrow. Call me i need to talk to someone about this

Harajuku Girls

MOM: Will your little cousin Nat like a Harajuku girls bag for christmas

MOM: It's cheap cause Im at Marshalls

MOM: Wait the harajuku girls look kinda slutty

MOM: Dad said no

MOM: BUT I LOVE GWEN STEFANI

Ina Garten

DAD: WHATS A CONTESSA AND WHY IS SHE BAREFOOT

XOXO

MOM: Guess who's super hot mom just spotted Blair's stepdad slurping noodles at a japanese joint in Chelsea. xoxo Gossip Mom*

*A deciding factor in choosing our fantastic literary agent was the fact that his fourteen-year-old daughter submitted this text from his wife.

TV Guide

ME: I'm bored

MOM: Star Wars is on spike. Princess Diaries is on Hallmark. Grease is on abc Family.

PG-13

MOM: Did you see the facebook movie

ME: Yeah . . . why?

MOM: You didn't tell me they curse:o

Disgusted

ME: Going to see the Justin Bieber movie!!

MOM: (:&)

ME: What?

MOM: That's my disgusted face. I hate the Beeb.

Backstreets Back

MOM: Just landed and had Brian Litttrlle from backstreet kids on in First class he said to tell my daughters hello he is so Nice

Ke$ha

MOM: How do you pronounce Ke$ha? Like Key"dollar sign"haa.

MOM: Or is it Key"dolla sign"haa, bc that's more hip? Call me and tell me!

Moulin Rouge

DAD: Have you seen Mallin Rougue?

ME: You mean Moulin Rouge?

DAD: Yea the one with the red wheel barrel and Nickole Kidman*

*There is no such thing as a "wheel barrel."

3D

ME: K, dad I bought the tickets.

DAD: better be for the 3d version.

ME: aren't we a little too old for that?

DAD: 3d or return tickets.

Impressions

MOM: How much???? (said like Borat)

Jersey Shore

MOM: Jersey Shore est gross

ME: So incredible.

MOM: snooki a mis ses foufounes dans le refrigirateur!!!*

Translates to:
"Jersey Shore *is gross.*"
"Snooki put her fanny in the refrigerator." ("Booty" is also acceptable.)

HARRY POTTER

Lauren: Each member of my family loves Harry Potter in their own way. My mom read it in book club; my dad listened to the books on tape. My sister, a fourth-grade teacher, discusses the symbolism with her students, and my brother, though he won't admit it, has read every one.

I have preordered the past three books and camped out at midnight for the designated "Kaelin copy." I get first dibs because I go to the bookstore, then it's passed to my sister, then to my mom, and then my brother will inconspicuously read the whole book cover to cover.

In the summer of 2005, *Harry Potter and the Half-Blood Prince* came out; I was about to be a senior in high school. I got to read it first. My house was very intense for a few days—every time I reacted to something I was reading, my sister would shout "DO NOT TELL ME ANYTHING!"

I finished, Dumbledore died, and—tears in my eyes—I passed the book to my sister. "DO NOT TELL ME ANY-THING!" Days later my sister was almost finished and my mom was anxiously awaiting the book.

"Something funny happened to my friend," I said. "He accidentally told his brother that Dumbledore died."

I cannot even begin to describe the looks of shock on their faces.

To this day, they still haven't forgiven me for that misstep.

We've been a little surprised about the number of texts that specifically reference Harry Potter, but I guess it makes sense. Families take their HP very seriously.

Dildodorf

MOM: Is dildodorf dead

ME: ROFL dumbledore is dead, yes

MOM: And snake man is dead also

Siriusly Great

MOM: Did you see the new harry potter movie yet?

MOM: I bought it the day it came out

MOM: It's SIRIUSLY great!!!!!

MOM: Did you get that last hp reference?

MOM: I replaced serious with Sirius

MOM: Funny, right?

ME: MOM, im still in school

Doopy

MOM: v r in the harry po movie. doopy is dead.

Horcruxes

MOM: In Harry Potter what did they call the 7 things that Voldemort hid his soul in? And didnt Dumbledore die from drinking that stuff Harry gave him with the shell?

Scar Face

MOM: Harry Potter out on video april 15

ME: weeee!

MOM: Would have been nice to see it in a theater z8) that's harry with his scar and glasses!

Hearing Aid

GRANDPA: I finished the harry potter movie. Couldnt hear half of it because my hearing aid fell out but it was visually stimulating. But not as visually stimulating as Avatar. What is Voldamert's purpose in life?

Dementors

MOM: i so so so tires

MOM: tired LOL

MOM: i feel like those things on harry potter that suck the life or soul out of you. except im not the sucker just drained man.

Hedwig

ME: looked at the apartment, second room way too small. harry potter room-sized small.

MOM: ok…. ill send you an owl…… (8> lol there

House Elves

MOM: Dobbie :(((((

ME: What?

MOM: Brain fart. Just sad abt house elves

Albus

DAD: Happiness can b found, even in the darkest of times, if one only remembers to tuen on the light. ~

ME: Words of the wise Albus Dumbledore. I am so proud

DAD: wow u r a muggle!

Harry Potter Guilt

MOM: Well I guess since you're an adult and a strong Christian, you could go see Harry Potter.

Muggles

DAD: I'm a Muggle!

ME: Do you even know what that is?

DAD: HP taught me

DAD: PS - I am magical....

Expelliarmus

DAD: Ungardium leviosa, ladies!!

ME: Do you mean wingardium leviosa?

DAD: It's levi OH sa, not LEVI oh sa

DAD: And by that I mean I booked the tix 4 HP land. watch out 4 expeliarmus @ college.

Practicin

DAD: Nevr insult Dumbleder in fron o me! Meant ter turn em into a pig, but i spose he wis so much liker pig anyway

DAD: I'm practicin me Hagrid voice

QUESTIONS

There are some questions you just shouldn't be asked.

26 CDs

DAD: Can you find the song YMCA by the village people and make 26 cd's of it for me by mid march?

Middle Name

MOM: How do you spell your middle name?

American Girl Doll

MOM: sorry to bother u. do u want your American doll 4 your kids? or donate? I respect your decision. Take your time to think about it.xox

A Website

ME: can you please go on whenparentstext .com? It's hilarious.

MOM: that's a website, right?

Discman Issues

MOM: Why does the music stop when I take the cd out?

The iTunes Store

DAD: would ya'll take me to the itunes store…i don't know where its located…is it on S. Congress?

One Eye

DAD: Have fun paint ball ing? remember that you only have one eye? be careful that no one shoots you in the remaining eye?

ME: Dad, i'm nearsighted in one eye, not blind…

DAD: You know what I mean? I would hate for you to lose vision? that would affect you for the rest of your life? how do you make a period on my phone?

Mail

MOM: Would you get the mail on your way in?

MOM: Mail please?

MOM: Could you get the mail?

ME: this is the only thing you ever text me about.

MOM: No. Sometimes I ask you to get the garbage cans too.

Yes

MOM: Do you want a baby fox?

Animal Hoarders

DAD: Does having beanie babies count as animal hoarding? If so we are guilty.

Netflicks

DAD: Why can't I find sebisquet on Netflicks?

Coordinates

MOM: where are you?

ME: home...

MOM: what are your gps coordinates?

Eye Troubles

ME: I just poked my eye out with mascara!

MOM: I hate it when that happens. Do you still have that pirate eye patch?

Cat Lips

MOM: Would it be weird to tell the neighbor his cat has nice lips?

ME: um....yeah.

Prom Date

ME: I think I'm about to get asked to prom!

DAD: Grace, will you go to prom with me?

PDF

DAD: L, could you PDF me a copy of your fall schedule? thx. luv, D.

Mambo Number 5

MOM: Ben, I want to download Mambo number 5 from itunes. how. love mom

Wanna Take a Ride

MOM: Listening to Lady Gaga's new song

MOM: What's a disco stick?

ME: Google it

Special 4 U

DAD: I would like to take you to the opera, music concert, symphony, whatever u wish and is special 4 u. "Shrek the musical"? Dana Carvey Live?Beach Blanket Babylon?

Beaver

MOM: Do you want to go see the Justin Beaver concert tommorow?

Shorty

MOM: Hey so some girls at work and i were wondering what a "Shorty" is, is it like slang for penis?

ME: umm no. not at all.

Yep, I Do

MOM: do you know what a choad is?*

*Google choad *or* chode. *For mature audiences only.*

Garbanzo

MOM: Have you ever noticed how much garbanzo beans look like little butts? Like being mooned by soup

Extras

MOM: what do u wanna get ur friendz for xmas? coffe cake? ice cream? hoop earrings?

ME: would my friends want any of those things?

MOM: not sure, i have extra in the basement

"Lesbian" Shoes

MOM: Dr Martens? Don't you already have "lesbian" shoes?

"U Know"?!

MOM: So, did u and Jon, 'u know'?!?

ME: Uhh, what?

MOM: "U KNOW"

ME: Mom, I'm not answering that.

MOM: Sarah told her mom.

ME: I'm not Sarah.

MOM: Maybe u should be. I'm telling grandma' that u did. She'll bug u. Then u'll tell me.

Ringtones

DAD: Jessie, when you get time could you send me some cool ring tones ? something like crickets or an angry cat, or some futuristic sounds. Anything thats cool or funny.

Boom Boom

MOM: Send me new music. I am bored of of these songs now.

ME: Ok, will make some CDs after my exam and send them

MOM: Also can you give me those Black Peas songs?

ME: What??

MOM: Those Black Peas - from that Boom Boom song

Parental Proof

MOM: What form of identification do we need?

ME: Just something to proove you're my parent. Like a birth certificate or something.

MOM: What if I'm not really your parent?

Two Questions

MOM: what's oxycotten?

ME: a drug mom.

MOM: what's a pearl necklace?

ME: we are not having this conversation.

Lost in Translation

MOM: What did you do with your sisters contacts, she can't find them

ME: I didn't touch her contacts, maybe she deleted them

MOM: From her eyes?

Shrink

DAD: your mother and I are having a marital problem. She won't let me sit on the new couch when I want to. She says that I need to use other rooms in the house. Comments?

Fashion Advice

MOM: Would u wear these MC hammer leggings

MOM: YA OR NAY ON THE HANGING CROTCH PANTS?!

Agenda

DAD: Could you meet with me for about 30 minutes to talk about:
-my website
-facebook
-other stuff

Quiet Floor

ME: Can't answer the phone- in the library. The quiet floor!

MOM: Never been there. What is the quiet floor? How boring? How are you going to meet any boys on that floor?

Hipster

MOM: Hey, what is a "hipster"?

ME: Lol, it'd take too long to explain over text.

MOM: You are one of them aren't you?

Slacks

DAD: How do you spell "slacks" (pants)?

ME: slacks

DAD: Thanks

SOS

DAD: Your mom is making blueberry pancakes. Now i just feel guilty that i am the one who broke her lamp. Do i tell her?? Choose __yes or __no. -Love Nervous Dad. :/ SOS.

Giardia

MOM: Hi, how are you feeling?

ME: A little better, Chris came down and took care of me.

MOM: Awww, that was nice, do you think you have giardia? What's with your sister and her FB pic?

ME: Uh, I don't know.

MOM: The one with the light saber.

Thankfully No

MOM: Did you ever see a kid pour vodka on their eyeballs?

Snow

ME: It snowed last night.

DAD: As in snow on Grounds ? Or Nose Candy at a party??

Conventions

DAD: just got stopped at airport for handwarmer in pocket. y must we all be so bound by convention?

Euphemism

MOM: Hey honey, what's up?

ME: Eating sausage. Requires both hands. I'll talk to you later :)

MOM: IS THAT A EUPHEMISM, YOUNG LADY?????

Naked Man

DAD: Why is there a picture of a naked man on the computer?

DAD: Is it from cock roulette?*

Dad has confused the website name of Chat Roulette, yet in his renaming he has captured the website perfectly.

PARENTAL WISDOM

Sophia: "My name is Sophia Fraioli," I said, slowly raising my fists in the air, "the greatest of all time!"

I took my place in the circle. This was not your typical preschool introduction. My dad turned to the other parents and with a laugh said, "Like Muhammad Ali!"

I grew up on the Lower East Side of Manhattan. My dad worked nights and would spend time with me during the day. Convincing me that my last name was "the greatest of all time" was only one of his unique forms of parental guidance.

I was the only girl in my playgroup, and my dad never wanted me to feel left out. Each day before I headed out onto the playground, he would look me in the eye and recite the same piece of advice: "Kick ass and take names." To this day, he uses those words whenever I'm in need of some guidance. And each time, I listen.

Text messaging allows parents to offer advice at every turn. For better or worse, these texts are some of the best gems of parental wisdom that we've received.

Meanwhile

DAD: I will deal with your sassy behavior wen I get home. Meanwhile have some fiber

Concerns

MOM: R U okay? I am worried. Sorry i couldnt talk had boys all to myself. It sounds like U have alot on ur plate right now. Please focus on what matters. I knowling you want to DJ, but please dont now. After you meet with your advisor, call me. I am playing Mah Jong right now. How bad is your lip? Sorry this is do long. Love, Mono

Flat Tire

ME: We got a flat tire..

DAD: Its only flat on the bottom.

Spidey Sense

MOM: Just watched a show. Be sure if your car ever breaks down or gets a flat tire, don't ever get out of the car. Call someone. Triple A or me or dad. Keep your doors locked and windows up. Not trying to scare you, but keep your spidey sense.

Nose Ring

DAD: i need to tell you something that's bothering me that you may not know. your nose ring is preventing many from taking you seriously. in fact it is taken as a sign of rebellion and immaturity. hence given the first impressions by those you encounter in life being skewed as result, the ring would actually be a hinderance. just as smoking is. do yourself a favor and get it removed. until you do, it will mostly be considered a character flaw

Facebook Reprimand

DAD: Use humor in a manner that is not offensive to others, and edit the language. Show some respect for yourself and family.

Love Dad

Dry

ME: My skin is really dry.

DAD: Well don't put it in the oven.'

Addict Help

DAD: Good morning! Hope u have a good time in Florida with your sister

DAD: One more thing, could u or please go to this site and just read this. The site is www .addict-help.com/marijuana.asp

Floss

ME: I got an A on my sociology paper!

DAD: Okay–be sure to floss regularly

Earmuffs

ME: I really need some earmuffs.

DAD: Just wrap a towel around your head.

Taking It to the Next Level

ME: What do you think of me and my friends buying an ice cream truck this summer?

DAD: Easy to get truck but very competative getting good route

Finals Advice

MOM: Good morning my little candy cane. Hope you had a good workout and yummy brkfst. Get your nervous poopy out before your test. Love ya.

Classy

MOM: Hi, please change facebook profile pic, delete beer pics and add Bible verse. Time to ooze class and brains.

Have Fun

MOM: Don't bite off the bad side of the apple. Have fun. Fall in love with everything.

Get 'Er Done

DAD: Tomorrow is the first day of your future yak yak yak and so on. no shit it really is, grit your teeth and get er done we luv you dad

Whipped Cream Vodka

DAD: what r u drinking tonight?

ME: whipped cream vodka

DAD: sounds disgusting

RIP

ME: Eww! Dad theres a mouse in the pool filter

DAD: Thats what happens when u swim alone, RIP mr mouse

Perceptive

MOM: Where r u?

ME: Strange folk concert...I'm in 5 inch platforms. Not my scene

MOM: Remember who u are!

Artichokes

ME: Do you know how long an uncooked artichoke lasts? Or how do you know if it's good or not?

DAD: Squeeze it and if it squeaks it's fresh. Thanks for asking these are the moments a father dreams of

Extra Careful

MOM: Be extra careful if you drive to the library as someone could reach through your window and unlock your door and hide in the back.

LOTR Wisdom

DAD: Gooood morning. Love you. Use your time wisely. Remember what Gandalf said. "All we have to decide is what to do with the time that is given us."

Box Wine

MOM: Have a great trip. Wish we were going. Stay away from box wine.

Hip Ratio

MOM: Babe, I really hope you're being extra careful with boys. Your hip ratio tells me you're going to be super fertile.

ME:...

ME: Please don't think about how fertile I am

Eye on the Cheese

MOM: Keep your eye on the cheese.

ME: are you drunk?

MOM: No!

MOM: Do you know what that saying means?

MOM: Mice in a maze will never stop trying until they reach the cheese. Metaphor for life.

From the Breakfast Buffet

DAD: ok. we need to get to sleep now, need to rest up for the breakfast buffet! love you!

ME: I'm jealous:(

DAD: study hard, save your money, marry well!

Nuts

ME: I can't believe Florida State just beat Duke.

DAD: Even a blind squirrel finds a nut once in a while.

Lessons Learned

ME: How was your day?

DAD: I learned that (1) customers don't like it when you ship them the wrong stuff and (2) one slice of ham on an egg salad sandwich is delightful.

Overshadowed

DAD: Never let your need to entertain overshadow your need to get work done.

Cool Kids

ME: Going out. see you later

DAD: K. Remember cool kids play water pong.

Waiting Room

MOM: when u crack ur knuckles do u know why it makes a sound?.. GHA trivia tv says… "escaping gases"…ewww..basically this means ur knuckles are farting!!..thts gross!

ME: still in the waiting room huh?

Hangover Speed

ME: Watching inception. Soo confusing.

DAD: Yeah the hangover is more your speed.

Great Expectations

DAD: I hope you are committing all the small crimes someone your age should be!

Church Guilt

MOM: So you didn't go to church today?

ME: Well I woke up, but then I fell back asleep.

MOM: Did Jesus ever go back to sleep?

ME: He probably did when He ascended into Heaven to rest.

MOM: Yes, from dying for your sins, just sayin.

Sperm

ME: im just having a really bad day . . .

MOM: just remember baby, at one time you were the strongest sperm.

The Good List

ME: Whats Good?

DAD: 1) It's a beautiful day 2) we are in FL 3) we are all together 4) we are healthy 5) we live in America 6) I have all my hair

Nothing Could Be Better?

DAD: what r u doing tonight?

ME: not sure really. there's a cookout at a church

DAD: free food and Jesus need I say more

IDEAS

Some of these are good ideas and some are bad ideas—you decide.

Leave of Absence

DAD: Just found out that the world record for balancing quarters on your forearm and catching them is 46. Just did 35 with little practice. Taking a leave from work.

Bridewealth

DAD: figured out how to help your love life. I'm trading you for seven cows. I'm going old school

Health Advisory

DAD: Don't get sick again this weekend!

DAD: Wash your hands!

DAD: And your mouth!

Band Names

DAD: Band name idea: Qualms

Recreational Turf

DAD: "Recreational Turf" sounds like a great class

ME: It's supposed to be an easy A

DAD: It might be interesting. Golf course turf, natural turf for football stadiums, etc.

ME: That sounds horrible..

They're BACK!

MOM: Did you hear?!!! FANNY PACKS ARE BACK!!! They're called "hands free totes" and they're the hottest thing in the New York designer lines for spring!! TRUE STORY! I heard it on the radio! So that makes it true. I'm just sayin…. Love ya baby!

Yankee Candle

DAD: You could poop your pants in the yankee candle store and no one would know.

Acting Career

DAD: I'm thinking of pursuing an acting career. My goal would be to play an autopsy corpse on NCIS. I know I'd have to start out small, like 1st I'd play a head found in a trash bag on a forensic documentary, then maybe a car crash victim in a medical training film, you know, work up to being diced by ducky. It's good to have goals...so I got that going for me.

Beasties

DAD: go to the doctor

DAD: get a pill

DAD: kill the beasties inside you

Not a Good Time

ME: i lost my voice

MOM: call me

Baking Soda

MOM: I forgot to call earlier to tell you that your feet smelled really bad when you were here to visit today. Try baking soda!

Jewish Spreads

DAD: Hi. hope all is well. ur pap smear results are normal…….. those 2 words sound wrong. pap smear. ill have a pap smear on rye!

Fire Safety

ME: The mall is on fire.

DAD: Get out.

Survival Advice

ME: Might not make it off the GW bridge alive in this storm.

DAD: Keep windows up if you go into water remember that car will float for a min till ya roll win down and swim away

Dead Fetus

MOM: found a band you could join called Dead Fetus

ME: That sounds terrible

MOM: but they're looking for drummers interested in heavy metal and jazz!!

Dryer.

MOM: ?

ME: what's up

MOM: Don't. Forget. To. Take. Lint. Out. Of. Dryer.

ME: ok

MOM: So. We. Don't. Die. In. A. Fire. Thanks

Giving It Away

DAD: Chocolate hot dogs. Million dollar idea for free!!

Destination Wedding

DAD: when you get married, I think you should have a destination wedding......IN BERMUDA!!!!!!!!!!!!

DO NOT FART

ME: I don't feel good. My stomach hurts

MOM: that's how I felt when I had that explosive diarrhea - be careful what you eat

ME: oh god ok

MOM: I'm so sorry you feel bad. DO NOT FART for God's sake. And if you feel the slightest rumble, go to the bathroom

How About That

ME: I need a pair of snow boots or something? my boots keep getting DRENCHED!

MOM: how about plastic trash bags

Extreme

ME: The boys that moved in upstairs are cool but they have a dog :(

MOM: Poison the dog and throw it out the window.

Spring Break

DAD: Hey, if you have the money & the time bring me back a cheap shell necklace, less than 10 bucks, that I can wear this summer… something that would look good with my tan. I'll send you the money back.

Father's Day Gifts

ME: don't know what to get dad for father's day

MOM: weight watchers membership

DISS

Sophia: The Fraiolis have been known to let the insults fly.

We make fun of my dad for his obsession with birds and his insistence on wearing a belt and suspenders simultaneously.

My family makes fun of me for stomping too loudly up the stairs. So much so, they've renamed me Heavy Step or Bigfoot. My eighteen-year-old sister is tormented for her inability to obtain a driver's license, and my mom's epic sneezes keep us laughing for hours.

When you're among family, no jokes are off-limits. But no matter how lame or insulting, a good diss between family members is almost always done with love.

Like, Oh My God

ME: We got here like, 30 minutes ago

DAD: like, great

Mama Jokes

ME: You're a bad texter.

DAD: yo mama

Subtitle

DAD: R

DAD: Sorry about that last message. Small keypad, old hands. Or whatever.

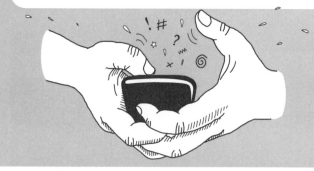

Txt Tlk

MOM: Lt me no wen u gt thr n b EXTRMLY CRFL!

ME: I'm pretty sure it took you longer to figure out how to shorten those words than it would have to just text the correct spelling.

MOM: Its txt tlk swee-t if i wntd 2 spll the hole wrds i wuld jst typ u a ltr.

Size 9

DAD: What size boots do you want me to order?

ME: 9 should be okay

DAD: 9 gonna give you the extra room?

DAD: For your stanky toenails?

Nonparticipant

ME: I called you back but your voicemail wasn't working.

DAD: don't send me text messages

Touché

MOM: My butt hurts from sitting in this darn chair!

ME: My uterus is trying to come out of my body. No sympathy from me. :(

MOM: YOU came out of my body. No sympathy from me.

Sharing a Room

ME: are you sharing a room?

DAD: Yes.

ME: with who?

DAD: My roommate.

No Reply

DAD: Where are you?

(no reply)

DAD: Your mother says WTF.

Ringtone

DAD: I set your ringtone as a crying baby, because it's annoying and it cries. Just like you.

Welcome Home

ME: You pick me up from college in 28 days!

DAD: Ok

ME: Yay would be a better response

DAD: Why do we get to drop you off somewhere else afterwards?

Environmental Awareness

MOM: Transferred grocery money. Deducted $50 for leaving on enough lights to power the state of Maryland. Jk but please be more aware

Graduation

ME: guess what! youre talking to a college graduate!

MOM: guess what! so are you

No Sympathy

DAD: SO ANY NEWS YET?

ME: NO, BUT I WILL LET YOU KNOW WHEN/IF I HEAR ANYTHING

DAD: ONLY CALL IF IT'S GOOD NEWS. I DON'T NEED TO HEAR YOUR TEARS

Cool New Website

ME: Hey dad, can you edit my term paper for me?

DAD: yeah sure, just send it to slavedaddy.com

Vodka Bottles

MOM: Can't find your shoes (the mocs) but I did see 2 empty vodka bottles.*

Oh, Snap!

DAD: you got a pkg from Costco today?

ME: what? maybe from amazon...

DAD: maybe. but that would require amazon to start with a C, end with an O, & have ostc in the middle. they both end with .com though.

*See "Pasta Recipes" in the Mealtimes section, page 109.

My Tone

MOM: Do you have any idea where the vaseline is?

ME: No, I don't live at home anymore.

(two hours later)

MOM: I don't like your tone.

Raisin Retort

ME: These raisins are gross

MOM: So are you HA

Mainstream

MOM: lobster in pot...kitchen is now crustacean station!!!

ME: ...crustacean station?

MOM: what....2 "mainstream" for u? ;)

Spinoff

ME: Gousjansnfjfdk

MOM: When drunk kids text

MOM: .com

Way Harsh, Dad

ME: I won my race :-) at least you have one child to be proud of

DAD: it only took you 19 years to win something

Your parents love you, and they'll never let you forget it.

Long and Strong

MOM: Love you long and love you strong.

No Socks

DAD: r u wearing socks?

ME: No im in bed why

DAD: bcuz when u wer younger id come in when u wer sleeping and rub your feet when they were cold.

Heart Happy

MOM: Do you and your brother see each other much?

ME: Yeah, sometimes we meet up for a drink and catch up.

MOM: Just the two of you? Just for fun?

MOM: That makes my heart happy.

Lupus

MOM: Make sure that these are the correct medicines that u are taking!

ME: They're antibiotics, I'm all set. Tonsillitis should start to clear up in a couple of days :)

MOM: Honey, I know u are nervous, god bless u.

ME: It's not that serious...

MOM: Did u get tested for lupus? Please know i am concerned & i am waiting for u to call me when u are done with the tests.

ME: It's tonsilitis.

MOM: U should fly home to be with your parents. This doesnt mean u failed in any way. Home means u have a place of comfort, a retreat, a place where u can get better while u get tested.

(ten minutes later)

MOM: Can u go in today and get results on lupus?

Pastor Advice

MOM: Pastor Dollar just did a great sermon on being single. Thought of you :)

Everything

DAD: How are you feeling?

ME: Not great. Throat hurts.

DAD: Sorry. Drink more emergency

ME: I'm doing everything I can. Nasal spray, cough drops, oral decongestant, vitamin c . . .

DAD: That a girl. I am very proud of you

ME: For using nasal spray?

DAD: Everything

Big Chance

MOM: sposed to be low 60's and partly sunny with a big chance of hugs!

Disney Play by Play

MOM: Turn on the TV! Beauty and the Beast is on!

ME: Mom. I'm at work.

MOM: Gaston's storming the castle! OH NO! He's stabbed the Beast! Gaston fell off the castle! The Beast is dying! THE LAST PETAL FELL! She realizes she loves him- He's rising off the ground- He's SO HANDSOME! And they live happily ever after. Love you!

Laugh and Smile

ME: :-)

ME: ok thanks mom lol

MOM: i like it when you laugh :-)

ME: well thanks:)

MOM: and when you smile:)

Less Than Three

MOM: Talk to you later 2.9

ME: 2.9?

MOM: You sign your texts <3

ME: and 2.9 is less than 3

Big Fat Wide Belt

MOM: Congrats! Another notch on your big fat wide belt!

MOM: Not that you're fat

MOM: Like a wrestler's belt

MOM: You know, one of those championship belts - only with lots of notches

ME: Please stop.

Heart Problems

MOM: 3>

MOM: damn. that didn't work.

MOM: how do you get the three to turn around

Oatmeal

MOM: I'm making oatmeal Cookies

ME: Why would you tell me this?! That's messed up...

MOM: because I miss you-I associate you with oatmeal

ME: Weird but thank you

Sure Is!

ME: Ok thanks dad! <3

DAD: What is that? a butt with a cone?.

Like a Virgin

MOM: How are you feeling today?

ME: Ugh. Cramps.

MOM: You should be happy, that means you aren't pregnant O:*)

ME: what face is that?

MOM: That's you, my virgin angel<3

ME: Thanks mom . . .

Nervy B

DAD: My love pls don't drink too much cause we saw a program on teen drinking and I got worried. Now I'm having a nervy b

Got In

ME: I got into the University of Michigan

DAD: love proud love proud love proud LOVE PROUD! !!!

Warning

MOM: Here's a poster they have against texting and driving: LOL, OMG, RIP. love ya

Means Love

MOM: #:-))

ME: Your smiley faces confuse me.

MOM: It just means love.

Forgotten

MOM: Hi honey. are you feeling forgotten?

Thinking of You

MOM: Thinking of u as i sit here eating a jar of sweet pickles i found in the back of refrig!!

Genes

DAD: :). Sorry for the bad genes. Love you so much!!!!

Easy to Please

ME: Hey, is it okay if I see a movie?

DAD: Yes.

ME: Thanks.

DAD: I'm proud of who you are

A LOT

DAD: There is still a bit you have to do to get the scholarship. Envelopes are at home. Love you both. A lot. I mean a LOT. Not just a little bit, but TONS! Do you get what I'm saying here? Are you picking up what I'm throwing down? Are ya with me?!

Back to College

DAD: mom cried because she saw the left over salmon in the fridge and she thought of you and how you love salmon

I. Found. U.

MOM: Its 3 a.m. where r u?

(20 minutes later)

MOM: Please let me know whats going on. R u ok?

(5 minutes later)

MOM: I. Found u. You r in bed. I didnt hear u come home. I was so worried! Glad we R all safe and sound. Love u.

Exclamation Point

MOM: love you exclamation point

GLOSSARY

Me: you should check out whenparentstext.com
Mom: here i thought it was a site that would help me

:-)8

*Bowtie Man**

+:)

Ash Wednesday

(\:D/)

Happy uterus

:()

Monkey

@(*.*)@

Monkey

He tweets, too. Follow him @wpt_bowtieman.

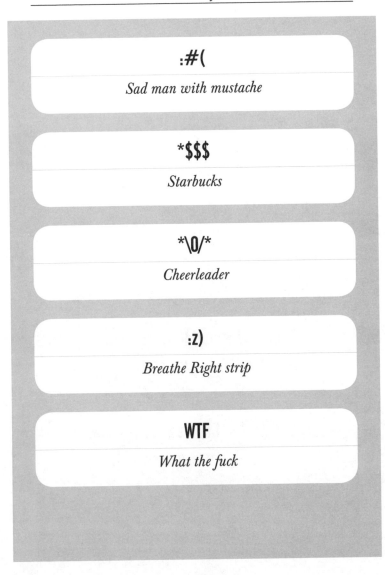

:#(

Sad man with mustache

*$$$

Starbucks

\0/

Cheerleader

:z)

Breathe Right strip

WTF

What the fuck

FML

Fuck my life

FYL

Fuck your life

:)=

Vampire

:1)}

Smiley with a beard

Chubies

How T9 spells bitches

(o Y o) —> (. Y .)

Shrinking nipples

3<]

Foot in ass

:-)3

Dimple chin man

:+)0 0

Party planner with balloons

({})

1. A hug from dad

2. A vagina

<3

1. A heart

2. A butt with a cone

3. Sideways woman's body

4. Sad ice cream cone

5. Less than three

)o(

Ice spider

)8(

Angel

(?_?)

Unamused face

@_____@

Froggie

(_/_)(__)(_/_)(__)(_/_)

Booty shake

:/)

Happy penguin

:P

1. *Tongue sticking out*

2. *"PLLLLLLLLLLLLLLLL"*

:{)-

Smile with mustache and under lip hair

#:-))

"Means love"

OoOoOoOoOoO

Popcorn

GGMM

Good golly, Miss Molly

:)B

Old boobs

:)8

Young boobs

```
  (\_(\
 (=' :')
(,(")(")
```

Rabbit

```
   (\_/)
   / . . \
 =\_T_/=
   /\.-.
   | _ |/
  / | | | \
  \)_|_(/
  ' " " " " '
```

Big cat

(:&)

Disgusted face

---

z8)

Harry Potter

(o)(o) & milk

1. Donuts and milk

2. Breast milk

~@~

A pile of shit

{:>(.

Sadness-distorted facial features

((((((((((name))))))))))

Cyberhug

A1

Waffles

B1

Muffins

BBM

BlackBerry Messenger

|L| |/

"I love you" in sign language

OUR FAVORITES

Sophia:

Tenderloin Sliders

ME: How's the bar?

DAD: Yes cool iron sculptures around the TVs

DAD: Has tenderloin sliders with horseradish sauce

Lauren:

Piece of Paper

ME: Can we go to yoga tonight?

MOM: Maybe - I really have to find a piece of paper on my desk, though, tonight . . .

ACKNOWLEDGMENTS

We have a lot of thanks and <3 to give. There are so many who have made our website and book possible.

First and foremost, to the thousands of people who read and submit to our site, thank you for sharing your texts with us. Your love for your families has made our website and this book amazing.

To our own families—thank you for your support and good humor. Thank you for making us laugh at texts and ourselves. To the Fraiolis (Eve, Tom, and Olivia) and the Kaelins (Marti, Mark, Matt, and Kristen)—thank you.

To our friends—the original fans, publicists, and critics of *When Parents Text.*

A special thank you to Julia, our dear friend, who coded the original five-star rating system while watching *Dante's Peak* in her attic.

To Zack, the best Web designer and coolest nerd we could ask for.

Thank you to both Jen and Amy, for your expertise and helping us keep it business casual.

To Judie, for being our advocate.

Thank you Bruce for your patience and editing wisdom; you have been an absolute delight to work with.

And to Brian, our wonderful agent and real-life bowtie man, thank you for making this book a reality. We would be lost without you.

275

ABOUT THE AUTHORS

Lauren Kaelin (right) and **Sophia Fraioli** (left) grew up in Montclair, New Jersey, and have been best friends since sixth grade. After graduating from Smith (Lauren) and the University of Vermont (Sophia), they moved back to Montclair and created the hugely popular website, whenparentstext.com. The two have since moved out of their childhood homes, but they still text their parents. They currently live in Brooklyn and make their own tacos.